Why Can't We Get Along?

Why Can't We Get Along?

Healing Adult Sibling Relationships

Peter Goldenthal, Ph.D.

John Wiley & Sons, Inc.

Published by John Wiley & Sons, Inc., New York
Published simultaneously in Canada

This publication is designed to provide accurate and authoritative information in re-gard to the subject matter covered. It is sold with the understanding that the publisher is not engaged in rendering professional services. If professional advice or other expert assistance is required, the services of a competent professional person should be sought.

ISBN 0-471-38842-4
Printed in the United States of America

10 9 8 7 6 5 4 3 2 1

Now Israel loved Joseph best of all his sons, for he was the child of his old age; and he had made him an ornamented tunic. And when his brothers saw that their father loved him more than any of his brothers, They hated him so that they could not speak a friendly word to him.

Genesis Chapter 37, verses 3 and 4

For my brother

Contents

Preface

Several years ago, I wrote *Beyond Sibling Rivalry: How to Help Your Children Become Cooperative, Caring, and Compassionate,* a book for parents of young and very young children who wanted guidance on how to prevent or at least reduce the nastiest sorts of sibling conflict.

After the book came out and I began the usual round of interviews and media appearances, I found that many people wanted to talk about their experiences in adulthood negotiating their relationships with siblings. When I met with groups of parents, most of whom had elementary school-age children, they asked me how to resolve everyday sibling problems. They also wanted to know what to do to ensure that their children would get along in adulthood. As one woman said, "I want my boys to be like Manasseh and Ephraim, not like Cain and Abel or Jacob and Esau. Cain killed Abel in a jealous rage. Esau, enraged when Jacob tricked him, first out of his birthright and then of his father's blessing, planned to kill his brother. Manasseh and Ephraim, two of Joseph's sons, are much less well known. This was exactly her point: we don't know about them precisely because they didn't feud. They simply got along.

Interestingly, most of the groups to whom I spoke also included a few grandparents. They spoke of their concern for their feuding adult children, some of whom were on the cusp of, or even in the middle of, middle age. It seems as if parents never outgrow their need to tend to the relationships among their children. For many years I have routinely asked adults in the families I treat in my clinical practice about their relationships with their brothers and sisters, and so have been very aware of how complex these relationships can be. The experience of hearing the same issues expressed by people all over the country convinced me that there was a real need for a book like *Why Can't We Get Along?*

❖   ❖   ❖

I also wrote the book because I believe that, contrary to popular wisdom, sibling rivalry isn't inevitable. If examples of feuds among siblings in well-known families abound, so do examples of affection and cooperation. Thomas and Raymond Magliozzi, also known as Click and Clack, the Tappet Brothers, have a very popular nationally syndicated radio show called *Car Talk*. Their show's popularity reflects two realities: people like to talk about their cars; and people like to listen to two brothers who so clearly enjoy each other's company. From speaking with people who know them well, I've been assured that their mutual affection is genuine and that running the car-talk business hasn't led to friction or to sibling rivalry.

Alfred Adler, the public health physician, psychoanalyst, and onetime colleague of Sigmund Freud, coined the term "sibling rivalry" at the turn of this century. He also wrote of the psychological impact of birth order. He, like Freud, was a brilliant man. His ideas have been seminal in psychology, psychiatry, and related fields.

Yet he remains a product of his time and place. While much that he wrote about remains true, there is much that needs updating. His ideas about birth order and sibling rivalry, for example, reflect the ancient tradition among European families of passing titles and property to firstborn children (typically male children) and leaving later-born children to fend, more or less, for themselves.

Similarly, generalizing too much from Adler's insights and trying to make them overly concrete can lead to all sorts of mistaken conclusions. It is not uncommon, for example, for journalists to ask me about the optimal spacing of children in order to avoid sibling rivalry. The answer to this question, like the answer to most questions about family relationships, is "It depends."

In addition, much of Adler's theorizing about sibling relationships has been distorted over time. Many of those who write about sibling relationships today seize on Adler's ideas about birth order, assigned family roles, and parental mishandling of sibling relationships while paying too little attention to the positive side of sibling relationships—to possibilities for future growth, and to the healing power of acknowledgment. I believe that Adler would be aghast to see that contemporary writers have gone no further toward explicating the causes and solutions of sibling conflicts than he did seventy years ago.

In developing my ideas about sibling relationships, I've endeavored to retain those of Adler's ideas that are relevant today, such as the impact of the birth of a second child on a firstborn. Where appropriate and helpful, I've integrated such ideas into my theory in ways that are consistent with my clinical experience and with today's world.

Finally, some of my motivation in writing this book was personal. I have one brother, who is eighteen months younger than I am. One of our family legends has it that my parents had planned a large family, but stopped after having two boys in such close succession. My brother and I were close as very young children, fought almost constantly in later childhood and adolescence, and had many conflicts as young adults. Despite the sometimes heated arguments, we both maintained a feeling of closeness. It was important to both of us that we remained true brothers in every sense of the word.

I feel very fortunate to have a brother who places as much importance on family relationships, and especially on his relationship with his only sibling. That is the reason I have dedicated this book to him and it is one of the reasons I hope to be able to help other siblings.

Acknowledgments

My ideas about family relationships in general and sibling relationships in particular have grown out of my study with Dr. Ivan Boszormeny-Nagy, the originator of contextual theory. Although the phrase has been badly overworked, it is a certainty that without him and his insights, this book would not have come into being. Lynn Seligman, my wonderful literary agent, understood what I wanted to do with the book, believed in it, and made a great match for it at Wiley. Tom Miller, my editor at Wiley, had a clear vision of the book from the beginning, and made many recommendations that have greatly increased its usefulness to readers. Lia Pelosi, also at Wiley, helped the manuscript through its final development into the book you hold in your hand, with professionalism and patience.

I was extraordinarily fortunate that my friend Roberta Israeloff was between writing projects at precisely the time that I needed her editorial expertise to help me out of a slew of organizational quandaries in the manuscript. As you read, if everything seems to flow along ever so naturally, the credit goes to her. Rabbi Alan Iser's discussions of what the Talmud says on the topic of Lashon Hara, the prohibition of evil speech, greatly enriched my understanding of gossip and the psychology of gossip. Finally to all the people, patients, and others, who shared their experiences with brothers and sisters with me, I would like to say, "Thank you."

Introduction

During the twenty years that I have been helping people to improve their family relationships, I have met many hundreds of people, very few of whom have been totally happy about their relationships with their brothers and sisters. Some had a vague wish for things to be better than they had been. Others yearned for intimacy of a sort they had never experienced. Some had not spoken to a brother or a sister for months or years.

Although very few of the siblings I have met were inveterate blamers, most were truly interested in understanding themselves better and in doing whatever they could to improve all their family relationships. They all wanted to figure out what made their brothers and sisters tick. As we worked together, they also learned how they might have unwittingly contributed to difficulties among their siblings, what they could do to improve those relationships, and how to let themselves off the hook if their efforts failed to produce the hoped-for change.

Lucy and her older sister Patty, for example, rarely fought—but only because they avoided relating to each other in any but the most superficial way. Neither was happy about this, but neither had done much about it. When Patty turned forty, she began to be concerned about what kind of relationship she would have with her only sibling when her parents were no longer around to pull them together. Thinking about this, she decided to reach out to her sister, to try to establish a closer relationship.

She called Lucy, who was vacationing at her lakefront cottage, and said that she would like to visit. After a few back-and-forth telephone calls, they set a date and made plans. Then, the day before Patty was to fly out to the lake, Lucy called to say that she had had second thoughts: she worried that Patty might not "go with the flow" at the cottage and that a disagreement or conflict might result. Patty said that she understood, that she wouldn't want to make her sister uncomfortable. But, in truth, she did not understand at all. While it was true that she didn't want to cause her sister any discomfort, the sudden change in plans had hurt her.

Patty was by nature a thoughtful, analytical person who tended to brood. She worried for months about the awkward telephone call and about her relationship with her sister, trying to convince herself that it didn't really matter. But it did.

One of her friends advised her to tell her sister off. Patty thought about calling Lucy and blasting her with the power generated by years of resentments. When Patty came to see me for individual psychotherapy, I asked what might be gained by this. She replied that it wouldn't serve any purpose; it would only make things worse. Yet she didn't know what else to do. She was on the verge of giving up, just accepting that she and her sister would never have a comfortable relationship.

However, I encouraged her to take a risk, not so much to change her sister but rather to assure herself that she had done all she could, that she had not let her hurt feelings and old anger stop her from reaching out. At first, she resisted this advice—as many people would. As children, we are all taught to follow the Golden Rule, or to "do the right thing." And yet as adults we often make decisions based on resentments and on vague ideas of what other people deserve. "She wouldn't lift a finger for me; why should I do anything for her?" thinking can dominate our lives and wipe out that earlier, more positive view of life and relationships.

Fortunately, Patty reconsidered her initial response. Though nervous, she called her sister and said, "You know, I was really disappointed that we weren't able to visit. I really hoped that it could be a time we could have had fun together and talked."

Lucy listened, but didn't respond. Naturally, Patty had hoped for a warmer response and was beginning to feel angry. After all, she thought, hadn't she been the bigger person? Hadn't she been the one to reach out after being let down? Couldn't her sister reciprocate at least a little bit?

If you are like most people, you can identify with Patty's predicament. Most of us who have siblings have thought at least once, "If only my brother or sister would just begin to act like a reasonable person, if he or she would show some consideration for other people, if he would not be so opinionated, if she was not so touchy all the time, our relationship would be so much better; I need to figure out a way to make him change."

But the reality is that we can't make anyone else change; we can change only ourselves. Once Patty remembered this—that she had called her sister to prove to herself that she had tried to improve their relationship, not to get Lucy to change—she felt better.

Although she was not happy with the outcome, Patty felt satisfied that she had taken action and that she had found a way to do it that was not blaming. By engaging in neither character assassination nor blame, she'd opened the door for future conversation. And while she still hoped for a closer, warmer, and more mutually supportive relationship with Lucy, she felt, for the first time, that she had taken a positive step, one that she could live with without regrets. The next time that the sisters were together at a family gathering, Patty felt much more relaxed.

How Will This Book Help Me?

If you have already made up your mind that your brother or sister is irredeemably bad, if you have totally given up on there being any possibility of a relationship, you will find little of interest in the following pages.

If, on the other hand, you're like Patty, and long to find a way to improve your relationship with your sibling—despite the fact that whenever you talk you find yourselves getting into childish squabbles, or walk away from nearly every visit nursing hurt feelings—then this book can help you. In it, you will find many ideas and specific suggestions to make changes in how you relate to each other.

The good news is that the techniques in this book have helped many other people whose relationships with their siblings have been difficult. These techniques do not, however, make the difficult sibling change. Instead, they give the sibling who is most interested in improving the relationship some ideas for self-change that may lead to changes in the brother's or sister's behavior. (The bad news, then, is that you, the sibling who wants change enough to read this book, will have to do most of the work.)

As you read this book you will learn:

- how to be more aware that your siblings' responses to you are less often in reaction to you as a person than they are to their childhood memories, marital satisfaction, and present psychological state
- how to increase your feelings of self-worth and self-valuation by doing more for your siblings and by being more considerate of them despite their selfishness, or perhaps even because of it
- that this same generosity represents the best sort of enlightened self-interest
- that giving siblings the benefit of the doubt and a second chance, even when you are quite certain that they will not respond, can actually reduce your anxiety, and in some cases reduce depressive feelings as well

- how to initiate a benign cycle by giving your siblings credit for trying even when their efforts do not produce anything positive right away
- how to give yourself credit for making these efforts, whether they succeed or not
- that you are not alone in facing these challenges
- how to accept what is, rather than continuing to grieve for what might have been

PART 1

Understanding Sibling Relationships

Chapter 1

Five Myths about Sibling Rivalry

Always do right; this will gratify some people and astonish the rest.

—Mark Twain

Who knows you better than your sibling? You grew up in the same house, share the same parents and the same upbringing, have many of the same memories. Yet few relationships can become as tangled and as difficult to understand.

You've probably encountered many situations in which your sibling's behavior seems to have had neither rhyme nor reason.

Amanda's Story: "Why Won't She Help Me?"

When Amanda came to see me early one Tuesday morning, she looked as if she had been up all night crying and then had done her best to pull herself together. Composed at first, within minutes she was in tears. Her widowed mother, Elizabeth, who had been in excellent health and lived very independently, had recently developed congestive heart failure and diabetes and now needed much more help from her children than she previously had.

Amanda, the oldest of three sisters, was married and had three children of her own, one of whom had developmental problems that required speech, occupational, and physical therapies twice each week. She was prepared to take the lead in helping their mother, but she was not prepared to do it alone. Her youngest sister, Roz, had just had a baby and so really was not able to help, at least not for a couple of months. Sheila and her husband, however, had no children and no other responsibilities. In addition, Sheila was a nurse with ten years' experience, so she seemed the perfect one to help sort through their mother's medical issues.

True, Sheila had never been exceedingly generous. But through the years, Amanda had been there to support Sheila, and felt confident that Sheila would remember this. She even told her friends, "I know that in a pinch, Sheila would be there if I really needed her."

But when Amanda called to ask for Sheila's help, she was in for a shock. Even though she just asked if Sheila could help out for a week or so, Sheila begged off. She explained that her time was taken up with helping her husband launch a new business. "I understand what you're going through," she told Amanda when Amanda explained how much trouble she was having juggling her son's schedule with her mother's needs. "I hear you; I know it's difficult." But in the end, Sheila said she couldn't spare a moment to help.

This hit Amanda hard. She had been counting on Sheila to help out during this difficult time. She also realized that she had perhaps not previously been able to see, or had not wanted to see, Sheila clearly.

What Went Wrong?

Amanda's story confirms a sad but unavoidable truth: there will always be times when despite your best efforts, your siblings will not respond to your requests for help, consideration, caring, or simple acknowledgment, no matter how fair those requests are.

Most people are like Amanda and try to be rational when thinking about how to explain an important issue to a brother or a sister. They also want to understand why a brother or a sister can't or won't respond to these requests.

When your brother or sister doesn't respond as you think a rational person should, if you are like most people you probably say to yourself:

- Did I explain myself correctly?
- Did I do something wrong in the past for which my sibling still harbors resentment?

You may also come to several conclusions along the way, any of which may seem totally justified at the time:

- He (or she) is a horrible person.
- Just wait till she wants something from me—I'll get even.
- I guess that's it; I thought I had a brother but I guess I don't.

Finally, you realize that you want two simple things:

- to understand why your sibling reacted in the way he did
- to be able to make him change, damn it!

But these desires are often difficult to satisfy, mostly because your expectations are unrealistic. In fact, there are many myths about sibling relationships and it helps to understand them more fully so that you aren't unduly disappointed.

The Five Myths about Sibling Relationships

Myth #1

If only I could really understand why my sibling behaves as he or she does, I'd know how to respond and then we'd have a better relationship.

Wanting to know why something happened or did not happen is probably as characteristic of being human as the ability to speak, having an opposable thumb, or being able to use tools. Biologists, chemists, and astronomers, and scientists in every other discipline, spend their lives trying to figure out why things are as they are, much to the benefit of us all. But trying to understand why your brother or sister acts as he or she does poses a much greater challenge than the kinds of questions that confront scientists.

Understanding your sibling and knowing what to do isn't rocket science: it's much more complicated and much more challenging than rocket science. Aeronautical engineers can be pretty sure that if they've worked the equations properly, things will go as they're supposed to most of time. You have neither formulas nor equations. And so it's unavoidable that you will be perplexed some, or even most, of the time by your sibling's behavior. Do remember, though, that neither you nor I will ever know with absolute certainty why our siblings act as they do. But even when faced with unanswerable questions, we can still try many different strategies to heal the relationship you have.

Reality

You may never know why your sibling acts as he or she does—
but that doesn't mean that you can't have a better relationship.

In fact, it is not necessary to fully understand why your sibling does something before you ask him to stop or tell him that it is annoying, insulting, or offensive behavior. Asking a sibling to change a behavior, verbal or otherwise, is not the same as attacking her character or being rude in any way. You are confronting a bit of your sibling's behavior, not her identity. And if your sibling accuses you of "character assassination," as Clarence Thomas accused the Senate Judiciary

Committee of "lynching" him, remember that people will say almost anything to defend themselves. It is up to you to calmly point out that their perception is incorrect: "I'm aware that this may sound to you as if I am attacking your character. I just want you to know that's not my intent. I'm trying to help you see what effect your behavior has on me."

Myth #2

The only way I can stop being so disappointed in and upset about my relationship with my sibling is for him or her to make some fundamental behavior changes.

Deep down, many of us believe that in order to feel better about our siblings and our relationships with them, *they* have to change. Amanda certainly believed that. She was convinced that when she called Sheila and explained how hard it was for her to care for their mother on her own, Sheila would say something like, "Oh, of course I understand. I'll come as soon as I can."

But all Sheila said was "I hear you" and "It must be so difficult for you." And as a result, Amanda was upset, disappointed, and angry. Her dreams were full of disturbing images and she was consumed by regrets. The phone call was a terrible mistake, she told me, and she wished she hadn't bothered.

Through our discussions, though, Amanda came to see that Sheila's failure wasn't Amanda's fault. She had made a good-faith attempt to reach out to her sister. It was extraordinarily important that Amanda come to see this, to appreciate it, and to give herself credit for it.

Reality

Sometimes changing yourself is enough to begin a process of change in the relationship. At the very least it can help you feel better about it and about yourself in that relationship.

Margaret was able to acknowledge this reality during a recent family gathering. It was Christmas Day, and she asked her brother Bill if he and his family would like to join her family for a trip to the museum the next day. Bill initially expressed interest but then said he'd rather wait to see what "everyone else is doing." In other words, he wanted to see if somebody else would make him a better offer.

Margaret explained that this could be a problem, because she planned to invite neighborhood friends to accompany her and her family if Bill and his family were unable to make it. When she didn't hear from him, she invited her friends. Several hours later, however, Bill called to say that he'd like to accept Margaret's invitation.

"Fine," Margaret said. "You can meet us and our friends there."

"I don't want to see your friends," Bill said, sounding put out. "We want to spend time with you."

Margaret could have gotten angry—but she didn't. Proud of herself for controlling her temper—for not telling Bill that his behavior was rude and insulting—she simply explained that she had made a commitment to her friends and wasn't about to cancel it. Bill then declined to go.

But a year later she was still stewing about how Bill had acted. She'd avoided a fight but had ended up feeling terribly resentful. Margaret came to see me because she had decided that she needed to learn to deal with Bill more directly in case a similar incident occurred.

The next year, when Bill and his family visited, Margaret again asked if he would like to go on an outing with her family, and again he replied that he'd like to wait and see. But this time Margaret spoke up. "It sounds like you are waiting to see if a better offer comes along, that you'd only want to spend time with me if there's nothing else to do," she said. "And I have to tell you, that doesn't feel very good."

Her response was direct; it held him accountable for what he had said but it wasn't offensive in any way. It worked, too. Bill replied that he'd not meant to offend, that he and his family would be delighted to spend the afternoon with Margaret and her family.

Myth #3

If my sibling tells me what's bothering her, I should listen carefully and accept her complaints at face value. After all, it's not right to question another person's true feelings.

Feelings, it's commonly assumed these days, are inviolate. What we feel can't be questioned.

However, it's dangerous to assume that your sibling's feelings, no matter how genuine, reflect reality. Mona, a woman with whom I worked, had a brother Jason, whom she described as very sensitive and totally insensitive at the same time: very sensitive about his feelings, totally insensitive about everybody else's feelings. As a result, he frequently spoke about his "needs," his "feelings," and his "perceptions" in a way that stirred up Mona's guilt and anger like froth on cappuccino.

My advice to her was to take whatever he said with generous portions of Morton's. I didn't mean that she should reject it all out of hand but, rather, that she needed to realize that Jason's feelings reflected only his reality.

Reality

Listening carefully is always important and valuable, but it's dangerous to assume that your sibling's feelings, no matter how genuine, always reflect a relational reality.

Your sibling's feelings reflect his or her personal reality, but that doesn't necessarily mean that his or her behavior toward you is always justified, or even accurate.

Myth #4

My relationship with my sibling is so imbalanced that we can never make it right.

One of the things that I have become convinced of after spending two decades of my professional life helping people understand and sort out difficult family relationships is the crucial importance of striving for a balance in giving and receiving in all close relationships, especially relationships among siblings. Although there can be lots of different interpretations of what "fair" and "unfair" mean, as well as of what level of fairness one ought to expect in relationships, I believe that most people would agree that the following family situations are grossly unfair.

• Mindy is the "giver" in her family. When her brother Hank was among those asked to provide testimony in a potential insurance fraud case at his hospital, he called Mindy once or twice a week, sometimes daily, for support. A year or two after the case was resolved favorably, Mindy ran into a different, but equally stressful, problem at work herself. She called Hank for advice, but he rarely had time to talk to her about it.

• Marti lived in the same town as her mother, while her sister Monique lived about two hours away. When their mother died, Monique said she would help Marti in any way she could. Marti then asked her to make some of the funeral arrangements. Monique said she would—but never did. Marti ended up making the funeral plans entirely on her own.

16

These are fairly typical cases of imbalanced sibling relationships. But there are many atypical cases as well.

I met with Silvio, for example, because he was concerned about his youngest son's poor school grades and sometimes insolent "attitude." Our discussions quickly turned to Silvio's very problematic relationship with his own mother and sister. Silvio was the oldest of three boys and two girls in what he referred to as "a very traditional Italian American family." After his father's death ten years earlier, Silvio's mother had chosen to live with his younger sister and her family instead of with him and his family.

Silvio was so hurt and angry that for years he hardly spoke to his sister. Unlike the many families in which the conflict is over who will "carry the burden" of caring for an elderly parent, in Silvio's family the issue was conflict over which grown child would have the privilege of taking care of their mother. This family's story shows that the important issue when aging parents need help is not always the "burden" of caring for a parent, but the resentment that comes when acknowledgment is lacking and one sibling's concerns are dismissed instead of treated with concern and fairness.

Reality

Most people interpret fairness in a liberal way, and don't expect a rigid quid pro quo. What they do expect, rather, is that over time those people to whom they have shown caring, generosity, and compassion (and this most certainly includes their siblings) will, if possible, find some way to reciprocate.

One of the best ways to remedy unfairness is to take a paradoxical approach. Let me explain what I mean by introducing Jenn—someone I never met. I learned about her from her older sister Pam, forty-three, who came to see me for a consultation. At the time, she was feeling extremely stressed because of her relationship with Jenn.

In Pam's opinion, Jenn, thirty-one, had been in an emotional downward spiral for the past year after losing her job and breaking up with her boyfriend. She spent most of her day sleeping and eating too much. She was also sponging off their elderly and widowed mother for her rent and all her other living expenses. Over time, their mother's savings had dwindled.

Although they were initially supportive and sympathetic, Jenn's three sisters and one brother soon began to think of her as "overentitled," a perception that was not helped by her whining and her feeling sorry for herself. The other four siblings were especially resentful of the way that Jenn continually complained that her deceased father and elderly mother had never done enough for her. Even when her mother agreed to pay for Jenn to return to school to earn a teaching certificate, her reaction was more one of entitlement than of gratitude.

Pam, her other sister, and her brother felt that Jenn should take care of herself and that she should not be going to their mother for handouts. Pam's initial questions to me were: "How can I get Jenn to grow up?" and "How can we get her to be more responsible, to act like an adult?" Pam said that she was embarrassed to admit it, but the truth was that she and her siblings were angry that their future inheritance was being squandered on Jenn.

I said, "Is there something you could do to help Jenn?" From the way Pam looked at me, I knew she was shocked by my question, which she found silly and offensive. Perhaps she even wondered if she'd called the right psychologist. Why should she want to do anything to help Jenn, who was busily grabbing everything she could?

But to her credit, Pam hung in with me and we began to discuss my question. I reminded Pam that she had told me that her sister was depressed. I asked Pam if she would like to try to help Jenn overcome her depression and thus feel better and have more energy. "If you knew what to do, if it was reasonable for you to do it, and if Jenn would accept it, would you want to try to help her?" Pam said that now that she knew what I meant, she would of course want to help her sister get back to her old self and, especially, get over her depression.

One of the ideas that emerged from our conversations was that Pam could stop being so constantly negative with Jenn. Pam did acknowledge that she thought Jenn would be a good teacher and that she would certainly enjoy it more than she did sales, a job for which she was definitely not well suited. I also suggested that Pam could talk with her siblings and encourage them to be more understanding and supportive of Jenn.

To Pam's credit, she took both of my suggestions. As Pam and her siblings saw Jenn's mood improve, and with it her interest in being helpful to them (she became very available as a baby-sitter, for example), they started to feel very differently and to look at the balance of fairness from a different perspective.

Descartes Was Wrong, or, Why It's Important to Pay Attention to Your Feelings

René Descartes was the French philosopher and mathematician who convinced the world that our minds and our bodies are two totally different and separate entities. But this notion that our experience can be divided in half, sometimes called mind-body duality, causes all sorts of problems. Some feelings, especially physical sensations such as fatigue, tension headaches, and stomachaches, become associated with our bodies. Other, equally real experiences such as worry, guilt, anger, concern, and compassion become associated with something we call our minds or our mental life. The truth, of course, is that mind and body are two inextricably linked aspects of life. Mental stress and physical stress are not two different things, but are, rather, two ways of talking about the same thing: stress. The rapidly growing field of psychoneuroimmunology has alerted many hard-nosed scientists to the ways in which what we usually think of as "mind" influences and is influenced by what we usually think of as "body."

Signs of Imbalance

When relationships are out of balance, the first indicator is often physical or emotional. Below you will find a brief checklist that you can use to identify emotional and behavioral indicators that your most intimate relationships are out of balance. For each question, ask yourself if your answer is never, rarely, occasionally, frequently, or always. As you go through the checklist, keep a tally of your reponses.

- Are you often tired in the morning, even after sleeping for seven or eight hours?
- Do you experience difficulty in falling asleep?
- Do you wake up during the predawn hours and find it difficult or impossible to get back to sleep?
- Do you find yourself snapping at your spouse or your children, often for no apparent reason?
- Do you often think of calling or writing to your siblings and then decide not to because you anticipate that the call will go badly or the letter will not receive a response?

- Do you become very frustrated or angry when your spouse, partner, or close friend acts in a way that reminds you of one of your siblings?
- Do you have feelings that your life is going nowhere?
- Do you have headaches?
- Do you have bowel problems such as irritable bowel syndrome or other intestinal discomfort?
- Is your appetite poor?
- Do you have trouble concentrating?
- Does your energy seem low?
- Do you have trouble getting going in the morning?
- Do you sometimes feel as if you had too much coffee when you've had none at all?

Scoring

Score one point for every "rarely," two points for every "occasionally," three points for every "frequently," and four points for every "always." Do not score "never" responses. If your total score is less than five, you are either remarkably stress-free or you are fooling yourself. If your total is between ten and twenty, you are experiencing levels of stress that are significant.

Myth #5

My sibling and I should be able to put our childhood differences behind us and just move on.

It's not uncommon to see brothers in their twenties or thirties fighting as if they're eight or twelve—never a pretty picture.

Sibling rivalry persists into adulthood for several reasons. The negative pattern of interaction that was established in your childhood becomes habitual after many years. Once we get used to relating to each other in a certain way, we do so automatically. And we keep on reacting in this way even though it seems out of character in our present lives.

For example, Felice, a woman in her early thirties who came to see me about five years ago, did not think of herself as lacking in assertiveness skills in most situations. That's why she couldn't understand her difficulty in being assertive with her brother Beau. During one of our discussions, she said, "None of my brothers or sisters ever confronts Beau, everybody's afraid of him."

"What are you and your brothers and sisters afraid of? What do you think he would do?" I asked.

"Probably start blubbering," she said, adding that she would be upset by his being upset. So her avoidance of a confrontation served to protect Beau, and to protect herself, too.

Felice's problem is much more common that you'd expect. Many people have siblings who retain the role they assumed in childhood. Perhaps, like Beau, they say, "Be careful with me. I may look and act sure of myself, but my feelings are very easily hurt." Perhaps your brother or sister was a truly sensitive child, one who became upset easily. Perhaps he or she discovered early in life that people in the family did not like the upset and would do almost anything to ensure that it did not occur again. Adults in the family might have become very tuned in to his moods so that they could appease him before he became upset. They may have trained themselves to notice very tiny cues—his tone of voice, small facial expressions, even the way that he sat or stood—so that they could anticipate his possible upset and act accordingly.

All this attention and accommodation would, of course, have been extremely gratifying to any child. And just as naturally, any child would, without thinking about it or even being aware of it, rely more and more on those facial expressions, tones of voice, and postures.

It's also true that family patterns that originally contributed to sibling conflict decades in the past tend to persist
long after the situations and stresses that led to them have
evaporated. Beau, for example, learned as a very young child
that the only way to get his depressed mother to notice him
was to whine and complain—to flaunt his feelings as a way of
saying, "Look at me, pay attention to me, love me."

Sometimes, though, the situations persist. If parents continue to unfairly favor one child over another, sibling rivalry
will continue whether the children are five or fifty.

(I will discuss several other powerful factors that can lead
to the persistence of sibling rivalry in Part 3, a sibling's emotional or personality problems. These problems and issues
can, quite independently of your behavior and regardless of
your motivation to make things better, make a warm and
supportive, or even a somewhat distant but supportive, sibling relationship impossible.)

Reality

Healing adult sibling relationships takes time and energy—
and the first step is acknowledging each other's reality.

In some families, though, what seems like an impossible
situation can be remedied if you accept the fact that sibling
relationships have to be worked on, and paid attention to, as
any others.

Kathleen, for example, was very distressed by her younger
sister Josie, who repeatedly said to her, "I've never gotten
over the pain of growing up with you." Kathleen initially was
upset and defensive, feelings that only grew when Josie detailed all the times during her childhood that Kathleen had
been selfish, insensitive, and just plain mean.

After several such conversations, Kathleen finally said,
"Look, things were tough for both of us; can't you just get over it?"

"I'm sure it was awful for her," Kathleen told me during our first meeting. "I was probably a nasty big sister, but can't she see that it wasn't my fault? She's talking about a time when I was really unhappy, too, but she can't seem to get that, no matter how many times I tell her."

I offered her an explanation that has been helpful for many people: "The first reason Josie keeps harping on the subject is that she's hoping for your acknowledgment of how bad it was for her. So far, you've been unable to offer this to her because you feel responsible. Complicating things further, your feeling of responsibility leads you to feel, act, and sound defensive. So as soon as she begins to talk about how horrible you were to her, you instantly start to explain that you weren't really so bad, that you didn't mean to hurt her and that it wasn't your fault. But all she wants is to 'hear' you say that you recognize her past difficulties."

The second reason, the one that lay farther beneath the surface, was that Josie had grown to rely on her feeling of having been harmed as a source of motivation in her life. It formed part of who she was as a person and what her identity was. She was "a person who had been badly hurt." When people build their identity in this way, it's no wonder they can't accept a sibling's protestations and explanations that things weren't really so bad, or that the sibling was just as unhappy as they were.

My advice to Kathleen was to stop being defensive. After all, she knew why she had acted as she had when they were kids. Their parents had gone through a horrible divorce, their mother had married again, very quickly, a man with very serious emotional problems and a strong tendency to be emotionally abusive—this is not a term I use lightly but it fits well here—especially to Kathleen. She recalled that he had threatened to kill her on several occasions. Her mother had been so detached from parenting that she had offered neither

PETER GOLDENTHAL, PH.D.

comfort nor protection in the face of the new stepfather's threats and erratic behavior.

Kathleen realized that she had almost certainly been clinically depressed from the age of eleven or twelve. All this made it clear to her that she had no reason to feel guilty or to defend herself. This realization helped her be free enough to give her sister what she needed: a compassionate and nonjudgmental ear. To be sure, Kathleen also told her how badly she felt for her, how she wished things had been better for her, and that she could easily see how her sister might think that she had hated her.

It turned out to be a very worthwhile conversation. For despite the fact that Josie had initially misjudged Kathleen, she was fully aware that their childhood was mutually unhappy. Despite her blaming language, Josie did not really feel that her sister could have done anything differently. After listening patiently while she recounted several incidents from their childhood, Kathleen said that she agreed that what she had done was horrible and inexcusable and that she had undoubtedly been nasty to her sister for years.

Then she asked a question that marked a turning point in the conversation and, ultimately, in their relationship: "What do you think I should have done differently?"

Josie's answer cleared the air: "You couldn't have done anything differently; you were just a kid." As the conversation progressed, other interesting things emerged. Josie clearly approached relationships differently than her sister. She was a strong believer in the "share every feeling you ever had, have now, or might have in the future" school of interpersonal relationships. Josie really believed that was the royal road to a better relationship with Kathleen. To her credit, Josie was able to listen when Kathleen explained that she had different ideas about what makes a good, warm, and mutually supportive sister relationship. It also became clear that she really did welcome feedback about her behavior. When Kathleen tried to test the waters by saying, "You know, you do most of the things you accuse me of," Josie nodded and said, "I know."

Kathleen came away with a new understanding—not only of her sister, but of how much time and energy was required to heal a sibling relationship. She also understood the importance of acknowledgment, a concept I'll address in depth in the next chapter.

Action Points for Positive Change

This chapter has offered a number of specific suggestions about how you can respond when your sibling's behavior confounds you.

Here are three you can post on your bulletin board or laminate and put in your wallet.

• Whenever possible, look for the positive motivation lurking beneath a crusty and negative surface. Even though it may not sound that way to you, your sibling may really believe that a statement like "I've never recovered from the trauma of your being my older brother" is a great way to open a healing dialogue.

• Remember that it is never a mistake to credit your sibling's positive efforts.

• If you think some of your sibling's behavior is designed to increase his feeling of self-importance or garner attention, find aspects of his demeanor and behavior that you like and, for those, give him the attention he craves.

Chapter 2

Acknowledgment Is Powerful

In my clinical work, I've been impressed again and again by how important it is for people to have those around them take note of the positive things they do or try to do. No matter what our age, gender, culture, religion, ethnicity, or profession, we all seem to share this quest for acknowledgment.

And our need to be acknowledged is often strongest in our closest relationships. It's not surprising, then, that we expect it most from those in our family, including our siblings.

Sarah's Story: "It's Okay to Ask for Acknowledgment"

One of the problems among siblings, however, arises because we're hesitant to ask for the acknowledgment we desire. We sometimes feel as if our siblings should magically "know" what we want without our having to articulate it.

Sarah, for example, spent many hours on the telephone with her sister Leah, including some late-night marathon calls, advising her about what to do to resolve her acute and very troubling marital problems. When we talked about this, Sarah recalled that she had not expected any thanks while Leah was in the midst of her marital crisis, but had hoped that she might say something later, after Leah's marriage had gotten back on track. The more time that passed without any such acknowledgment, the more Sarah became aware of her resentment building. She did not answer the phone when she thought it was Leah, and did not return calls when Leah left messages.

Then she decided to talk to Leah directly about the acknowledgment she wanted. Leah's first reaction was surprise. "But I thought I told you how much I appreciated your help," she said. "I never could have made it through those months without your support." Then she said, "Maybe I just thought I told you. You know, I was so wrapped up . . . I'm really sorry. You must have thought I was unappreciative." Sarah said it felt wonderful to hear this. She only wished she had asked Leah about it sooner.

Indirect Requests for Acknowledgment

Nothing feels better than acknowledgment asked for and bestowed. But relationships aren't always this straightforward. In fact, many people rarely come out and say what they want. Instead, they ask for it in all kinds of indirect ways. Here are three examples. See if any of these siblings remind you of yours.

Wally's Story: "He's So Self-Absorbed!"

Wally Lockman's younger brother Kevin took one of those weekend "trainings," the sort that claim to help you get in touch with your feelings and learn to achieve greater intimacy. After just one session, Kevin was a total convert to the training style of life. Wally was not impressed by his brother's insights, nor was he interested in being converted.

In fact, he was bored by his brother's almost unfathomable depth of self-fascination and self-preoccupation, which the training seminar seemed only to have heightened. "You keep talking about how these 'seminars' help you become so much more aware and sensitive," he said to Kevin. "But are you aware that we have been sitting here for nearly an hour and you haven't asked me a single thing about how I'm doing, about my family, my vacation plans, my work, anything? I think you were much more spontaneous and fun before you started these things."

Next, because Kevin was involved in a pyramid scheme, Wally tried to show him how foolish he was being, throwing his money away on this. "I mean, it's obviously a great moneymaker for somebody," Wally said. "Maybe you should invest in the business instead of giving them your money."

Kevin was neither pleased nor amused. He was so offended, in fact, that a very icy period followed Wally's heartfelt attempts to rescue his brother from expensive silliness. When Wally came to see me, upset about his relationship with his brother, I asked him to consider the possibility that Kevin was probably looking to him for some kind of approval. "That's a real possibility," Wally admitted. Next, we talked about how he might better respond the next time the subject came up and what he might say that would be positive without being phony.

After relations had thawed, Wally tried this new approach. The next time Kevin started talking about his recent self-discoveries and the benefits of the "Learn-to-Love-Your-self" seminar he had recently attended, Wally said, "You know, Kevin, even though it isn't how I would choose to spend a weekend, I admire you for your openness to new ideas." Wally wasn't sure how this would go over, but it was true, so he said it.

Much to his relief, Kevin was not only genuinely pleased, but talked about it less for the next half hour or so. He was even able to step outside himself long enough to ask about Wally's tennis game and his recent vacation. Wally told me that he did not quite understand how it worked, but that he intended to continue to look for ways to acknowledge his brother, since it seemed to at least temporarily bring him back to earth.

As it turned out, all Kevin wanted was for Wally to acknowledge his efforts. He didn't know how to ask for this directly, though; Wally had to figure it out.

This is often the case. In fact, sometimes siblings asking for acknowledgment go about it in very off-putting ways.

Linda's Story: "He's So Stuck Up!"

Linda had recently taken up tennis and was talking with her brother Zach, who had been an avid tennis player since childhood, about her newly discovered passion for the game. "Maybe we could play sometime," she said, "and you could give me a few pointers."

Zach's response was not at all what she expected. "You need more lessons first," he told her. "I've played for so long I wouldn't know how to play at your level. You need a teacher, not a tennis partner. Work at it for six months or so, then maybe we can hit a few." Linda was disappointed and annoyed.

Then she remembered the rule of thumb we had discussed: a brother's boastfulness often disguises his wish for acknowledgment. With this in mind, she said, "Zach, I know I can't play at your level—you're so far ahead of me. But I was sort of hoping you could help me by being what you said I needed, you know, a teacher; I mean, if you have time."

Linda knew that her intuition was correct when Zach softened: "Well," he said, "maybe I could show you the strokes, help with your grip, that sort of thing—but we couldn't possibly play a game."

Joe's Story: "He Can Be So Hurtful!"

When Joe's younger brother Keith bought the sailboat of his dreams, the kind that he could sail around the world, Joe experienced a range of emotions. He was impressed that his "little brother" had been so successful in business that he could afford so expensive a toy. He wondered if Keith would invite him to go sailing. He also wondered if he perhaps had made the wrong choice when he'd decided to become a public defender, since his work provided neither the income to purchase a boat nor the leisure time in which to use it.

Keith began to talk about his grand plans to sail to the South Pacific, if not around the world, and suggested that Joe "take six or eight months off, get a boat, and sail with us." Joe initially felt that this was intentionally hurtful, a way of pushing the point that Keith was rich and able to leave his business to run itself for a year or so while Joe was a working stiff who was grateful for his three weeks of vacation.

After we talked about this incident, Joe realized that Keith had not intended to insult or hurt him, but was, rather, aching for acknowledgment. So Joe gave him what he needed. He told Keith how impressed he was about the boat, and about the great sailing adventure. Then he added, "I wish I could do something like that; maybe someday if I figure out a way to be as successful as you are, I'll be able to."

As I thought he would, Keith changed his tune. Modestly, he referred to his own "good luck." Because Joe had given Keith the acknowledgment he needed, Keith was free to admit, "You know, Joe, it's nice to be able to take a lot of time off from work, especially if your work is not all that fulfilling, but I'd trade it for having a job that I really loved."

Wally, Linda, and Joe could have reacted very differently. They could have lectured their brothers, or become egocentric or nasty themselves. And who could blame them? When your brother sounds as if he is so taken with himself, his accomplishments, and his challenges that he forgets you are a person, too, the last thing you may want to do is to find something positive to say to him.

But the reality is such that if you react this way, what you'll probably meet up with is escalating conflict, cold-war standoffs, and bad feelings all around.

To avoid this, try something different, even if it seems unnatural at first. The best way to help your siblings see the value of acknowledging your accomplishments and your efforts to be helpful to them, to your parents, and to others in your family is to show them how good it feels to receive acknowledgment.

You may also feel that offering acknowledgment in the way that I am suggesting begins to feel like a parent offering approval. But in reality, few people totally outgrow a desire for approval from family members, not just from parents, but from siblings as well.

Changing Your Reactions

Try this exercise the next time your brother or sister:

- seems so self-absorbed as to be unaware of you as a person
- puts you down
- boasts or acts like a show-off

Instead of following through on your first reaction, which is probably to get angry, take a deep breath and hold your anger at bay. Instead, ask yourself:

- Does she want me to recognize her?
- How can I give him credit?

Actively Search for Positives and Ways to Give Credit

It is all too easy to be swept up by a culture of blame in which we are quick to notice our siblings' shortcomings and slow to recognize their contributions and accomplishments, if we notice them at all. Even if you are one of the many people who are highly critical of themselves and other people, you can learn to exchange your natural inclination to scrutinize siblings for possible blame for an active and energetic commitment to looking for things to praise and acknowledge.

Start with the most obvious and easiest to remember: acknowledge those things that your sibling does or says that are, or have been, helpful to you or to someone else in your family. Look for the little things that happen every week or every month.

Small gestures speak loudly

Acknowledging your siblings' efforts to be helpful, even when the result of those efforts is far from perfect, is as important as acknowledging what they achieved or did for you or someone else in your family. These gestures can be mundane, such as thanking your sister for a birthday card even though it came a month late, or thanking your brother for offering to take your four-year-old to see a newly released horror movie even though you are certain it would scare your child half to death.

The efforts you may wish to acknowledge may also be interpersonally intense and layered with meaning. You may want to thank your sibling for her thoughtfulness in offering to help you find a psychologist or psychiatrist to help with your work-related anxiety even if you do not want this kind of help.

Take Drew, for example. During his consultation with me, we soon began talking about his brother Greg and their unhappy relationship. Greg, who had been overweight and out of shape for many years, finally put himself on a diet, joined a local health club, and started to exercise three times a week. He felt great, and with the zeal of a reformed junk-food addict, told his brother Drew about his new way of living. He also could not resist suggesting that Drew, overweight and sedentary, should do the same.

Many men in Drew's position would have told Greg to mind his own business. This was Drew's position—at first. As he put it, "Before we started talking about this stuff, I would have told him to leave me alone and stop showing off."

But because of our talk, he took a different tack. To his very great credit, he thanked his brother for the advice, adding that he was probably right. When a friend said to Drew, "Why do you let your brother talk to you that way? He's not perfect!" Drew's answer was characteristically practical:

"How would it help to get angry? He thought he was helping."

The Difficulties of Giving Advice

Sometimes the request for acknowledgment comes as a request for advice or in the form of a suggestion. Trouble often arises when one sibling receives what she perceives as uninvited and perhaps unwanted advice (older brothers and sisters are especially likely to do this).

Most of the time, this advice is well intentioned. I am not trying to convince you that it is always good advice, only that you should not assume that because it may offend you, it was designed to offend you. Remember, it does not cost anything to acknowledge your brother's or sister's desire to offer you some helpful advice. Don't be cloyingly sweet about it, and don't say, "Thanks," for things that seem wrongheaded or hurtful. Rather, look for an opportunity to give them credit for what they gave you that was positive.

Here are two women who figured out how to do this.

Naomi's Story: "Let's Think of Another Way"

Naomi and her sisters were talking about doing something special for their father's birthday. Kathleen, who was living on the other side of the country, suggested that Naomi pick him up at his home and drive him to and from work each day for a month. Naomi told me her first reaction was that this was an outrageous suggestion: "Let Kathy fly out here and be his chauffeur for a month!" she thought to herself.

Later, after letting off some steam and having had time to consider her options, what she actually said was, "Kathy, I'm sure he'd enjoy being pampered that way, but I'm much too busy to drop everything every morning and again every afternoon. Maybe we can think of something that will make him feel just as special that we can all contribute to."

Samantha's Story: "Would You Like to Help Me?"

Samantha planned to write and illustrate a book about flower arranging based on the many elaborate arrangements that her mother, Florence, had made for holidays, family events, and other special occasions. In Samantha's mind, it was to be a tribute to her mother's creativity and a way of memorializing her.

Samantha envisioned only one impediment to completing her project: all the notes and drawings had been stored in her sister Heather's attic. For as long as she could remember, Samantha thought of her sister as someone who tried to control everything and everyone around her. She anticipated that Heather would either not want to let her have the materials or would try to "steal" the idea of putting a book together.

Samantha talked with a friend about her predicament and came up with what seemed like a novel plan: she asked

Heather if she would like to work on the project with her. Heather was delighted. She thanked Samantha for asking her, and threw herself into it.

Heather's reaction so surprised Samantha that she wondered why she'd been so afraid to approach Heather in the first place. Had she been wrong about Heather for all these years? Had Heather changed? Or was it simply that Heather appreciated being acknowledged? We'll never know. But we do know that both Naomi and Samantha found ways to work around the roadblocks their siblings had erected, preventing what could have been terrible arguments.

Enlisting your sibling's help in solving a problem can save many relationships.

Treat Your Sibling As You Would a Friend

Many of the strategies I described above should seem pretty familiar to you. You probably rely on them often when dealing with friends. Unfortunately, we tend to treat our siblings more harshly than we do our friends. When we become frustrated or disappointed in our siblings, it's so easy to flip back into childhood patterns of mutual taunting, being overly sensitive, and stubbornly refusing to back down. While we are used to treating our friends with self-restraint, tact, and a sense of humor, we often forget to use these techniques with our siblings.

One of the reasons for this is that we understand that our relationships with our friends and our coworkers are mutually elective: friends can drop us at any time if we become too difficult to deal with. Coworkers can try to avoid interacting with us. Our brothers and sisters are stuck with us, no matter how much we might overreact to something like an innocent joke. They are stuck with us, but they do not have to like it. The more that you can learn to respond to your brother's or sister's positive intentions first, the better things will be between you.

Jackie's Story: "He Thinks I'm Bossy!"

Even if your sibling is extraordinarily selfish and self-preoccupied, he or she will begin to respond positively to your acknowledgment. Jackie, for example, originally came to see me for help in reducing the conflicts among her children, but our work soon focused on her relationship with her brother Lenny. Lenny's motto was: "Nobody can push me around." In other words, if anyone asked him to do something, he'd refuse. He couldn't even bear to give Jackie a lift to the gas station if he felt it was "expected" of him.

As a result, an icy coldness grew between Jackie and Lenny. He wanted to be closer to her, but worried that if he were to accept even partial responsibility for the tension between them, he would be giving in. When he tried to talk with her about this longing, he fell into his old blaming: "The reason we are so distant is that you're so bossy; I never know when you're going to jump all over me. I can't let anything get by me, because then you'll start taking advantage of me."

Jackie's immediate reaction was to think to herself, "He's got a lot of nerve blaming me for being bossy!" However, unlike her brother, she was willing to accept some responsibility in the interest of trying to improve their relationship. So instead of trying to defend herself by denying that she was bossy or domineering, Jackie said, "Hey, that's a surprise. I always thought you enjoyed asserting yourself. I thought you just liked being a 'toughie.' I never knew you felt that I was the bossy one. I guess we've been feeling the same way all these years."

This one remark diffused the tension between brother and sister considerably—not forever or even for very long, but for the next several days. And that was a step forward. An even greater benefit was that Jackie now knew she had a tool that she could use to get through some of the awkward and tense moments that were sure to arise regularly in the future.

When you are in the midst of a difficult discussion or argument with your brother or sister, it's natural to react quickly, forcefully, and emotionally to what they have said that you dislike. This is another of the aspects of sibling relationships that makes them different from other relationships between adults. In most social and especially work situations, in which we have to continue working together, we have all trained ourselves to bite our tongues from time to time, to ignore quite a lot of what some coworkers and many superiors have to say to us, and to try to smooth out differences.

It's a good idea to bring some of this perspective to our dealings with our siblings.

Recognize Their Difficulties, Too

Sometimes, siblings go through a difficult phase in their relationship because one of them is having a problem and doesn't know how to talk about it.

Laurie, for example, told me that she was completely disgusted with her younger brother Nick's hypercritical comments and extraordinary narcissism. It seemed to her that every time they talked, Nick had a new complaint about her, a new way of putting her down, or a new way of comparing himself to her. He never had been particularly gracious, but his manner over the past months had been almost insufferable. From greeting her with comments such as, "I see you've put on a little weight," to making disparaging comments about her choice of wallpaper, everything he said seemed calculated to hurt.

Since Nick was an investment adviser, she asked his advice about getting a bank loan for the small home-based business she hoped to start. When Nick blasted her idea, telling her that it was entirely without merit and that she knew nothing about making money, she was furious and devastated. It had been a huge mistake, she realized, to even raise the subject with her brother.

My advice to Laura was to assume that Nick wanted something from her and that she needed to try to figure out what that was. I also reminded her: "When in doubt about what to say, look for something to acknowledge."

Some time later, Nick mentioned that he and his wife were searching for "the best private school for little Nicky." Laura quickly realized that he expected her to be interested and supportive, which was more than she could bear. To her way of thinking, her brother's desire for "the best" private school was just one more example of his status seeking.

But then she remembered my advice, and figured it was worth trying. "I guess looking for a school for little Nicky has been stressful for you and Louise," she said. "Is there anything I can do to help?"

Nick responded by telling Laura the reason for Nicky needing a special school: he had been found to have developmental problems and was not learning to read. Nick hadn't brought this up before because he'd been "too upset to talk about it."

Laura's offer to help gave Nick a chance to unburden himself of worries he had kept to himself for many months. It also led to a surprising, albeit temporary, change in Nick's demeanor. After they had talked about Nicky for some time,

Nick actually asked Laura how her business plans were coming along and offered to help her with them if she wanted him to. Laura felt that this was a positive sign, even though she realized there was a chance he would forget about his offer to help.

Acknowledging your siblings' past and present difficulties and struggles, as well as the obstacles they have faced in their lives, helps avoid conflicts and fosters interpersonal healing. It is remarkable how frequently a brother or a sister will come across as just plain nasty until you say something that recognizes their struggles and stresses.

Don't Be Afraid to Apologize

The words "I'm sorry" seem to be disappearing from our vocabulary. But sometimes offering an apology is the most healing thing you can do—and a special form of acknowledgment in itself.

Barbara, Felicity, and Sheila decided to plan a big party for their parents' fortieth wedding anniversary. The plans were complicated by distance: Barbara lived in Chicago; Felicity had been sent to England for a year by her company; Sheila lived in Los Angeles. Each sister wanted the party to be really special. Each had many pressures in her own life. During one of their conference-call planning sessions, Felicity said that she would like to have oysters for an appetizer. Sheila, whose husband had developed hepatitis after eating some bad shellfish several years before, objected, saying that it would make her uncomfortable. Felicity said, "So what if you're a little bit uncomfortable? Our guests' enjoyment is more important than your feelings!" Sheila hung up in a huff; Felicity and Barbara continued to discuss the party for several more minutes. Felicity was upset, but felt that her sister had overreacted.

The next day, Felicity continued to be distressed about the difficult exchange of words with her sister. She still felt that Sheila had overreacted, but wanted to do something to smooth things over. At my suggestion, she called Sheila and said: "You know, I didn't mean anything personal by what I said. I'm really sorry about the way it came out. I didn't mean to hurt your feelings." Sheila accepted the apology graciously. She admitted that she had felt hurt and that the apology did a lot to restore her good feelings about Felicity and about the party they were planning.

This vicious cycle of hurt and resentment—which Felicity managed to break with her apology—characterizes many sibling relationships. One sibling's inadvertently hurtful remark sparks a brother's or sister's caustic comeback, or perhaps their smoldering resentment. The resentment later emerges as a put-down, as a bit of sarcasm, or as a snub. More resentment, and more hurtful remarks, follow. At best, all this continues in the background, undermining what might otherwise be a solid and mutually supportive relationship. At worst, it reaches a critical mass and leads to a fight or perhaps a long period with no contact between brother and sister.

No matter how much we try to avoid it, each one of us does things that cause other people emotional pain. We forget promises, we lie, we are insensitive. If we don't do anything to try to rectify these mistakes, they will inevitably make that vicious cycle spin faster and faster. But a simple apology followed by a sincere effort to avoid a repeat of whatever you said or did that hurt your sibling can stop the cycle. It may even start a spin in the opposite direction. Many siblings will think, "If he can be big enough to admit he was wrong, I can too."

❖ ❖ ❖

FACTS ABOUT APOLOGIES

- Apologizing is not a sign of weakness: it is a sign of strength. The person who can recognize and acknowledge her own mistakes is almost always the psychologically healthier person in any close relationship.
- Saying you're sorry for something that you did or said, forgot to say, or forgot to do is not the same as admitting that you are a bad person or that everything is always your fault.
- Sibling relationships (and other close relationships) are different from business relationships. In business, people often worry that someone will see them as weak and try to take advantage of them if they admit their mistakes. I am not convinced that this is actually true even in business, but it is definitely not true in families.
- If you are wondering whether you should apologize for something that you said or did, failed to say or neglected to do, you probably should. There is much to be gained and nothing to lose.

Recognition Is Acknowledgment, Too

Sometimes, what siblings are looking for from each other is simple recognition of themselves as people.

Sue, for example, told her brother Max that she could not come to his fortieth birthday celebration if it was on a Friday night because she didn't drive on Shabbat. Max was incredulous. "Come on!" he said. "You've got to be kidding me! It's my birthday!" Even when Sue reminded Max that she was not kidding at all, that she really did observe the Shabbat prohibition of work, and driving or riding in a car, Max pressed the point by saying, "I don't believe it. You're putting me on."

Sue, Max, and their sister Rachel always identified themselves as Jewish in the way that many American Jews do. When they were children, their parents belonged to a synagogue, supported Israel, and attended services on Rosh Hashanah and Yom Kippur. Jewish identity was important; religious practice was not. Sue, her parents, and her siblings were, she assumed, Americans first and Jews second.

Because her identity as a Jew was important, however, she and her husband joined a synagogue so that their five-year-old son Adam could attend Hebrew school. Sue began to attend services mostly to set an example for Adam. One thing led to another and by the time Adam was seven, she had, in fact, become an observant Jew. She was still self-conscious about the way that her observance set her apart from many of her friends, from her coworkers, and most of all from her parents and siblings.

Max's insensitivity and mocking tone hurt her deeply. At first she was embarrassed to confront her brother about this. After all, she thought, his was the dominant view in her family. She wondered if she should make an exception for his party. Then she realized that she would resent doing that, not just because it would mean giving in but because it would be like agreeing that her values had no merit. Although she was nervous and avoided talking to him about it, she felt greatly relieved when she took him aside and told him about her observances and asked him why he had reacted as he did.

Much to her surprise, it turned out that Max had assumed she would make an exception for his party. He also confessed, "I guess I'm not really comfortable with religiosity." Their conversation was not particularly heavy or even very long, but it was enough for them to arrive at a workable compromise: Sue and her family would arrive for the party before sunset and would stay over through Saturday. As a result, Sue felt that her brother had seen and acknowledged her and her values.

Action Steps for Positive Acknowledgment

Acknowledgment, for all its value, does not come naturally for many of us. Here are some steps you can take to heighten your awareness of the importance of acknowledgment:

- Actively look for opportunities for acknowledgment. Learning to acknowledge your sibling's positive contributions and efforts is like looking for wild strawberries. It can be a challenge to find the first one amid the grass and the weeds, but after you get some experience in identifying their shape and color, you begin to see them poking up everywhere.
- Be positive. Don't make it up, but if something positive is happening, be sure to say so. Before you tell your brother that he is playing too roughly with your three-year-old, tell him how much it pleases you that he comes over to spend time with his nieces and nephew. Ask yourself, "How will it help to get angry?"
- Give credit for efforts, not just for outcomes. Has your sister been trying not to interrupt you so much? Did your brother offer to clear the table after a family celebration for the first time in a decade? If you carp that she still interrupts, or that he didn't wipe the table thoroughly, you'll wait a long time for repeat performances. If you can notice their positive efforts, however, you will be sure to see more of them.

44

- Remember the Golden Rule. If you are unsure about just what is the right thing to acknowledge in your brother or sister, give them credit in a way that you would want them to give credit to you.
- Don't limit acknowledgment to big things. Acknowledge the little things, too. If your sister gets engaged, makes partner at her law firm, or wins a national prize for her photography, everybody will be lining up to congratulate her. You may be the only one to notice her patience with her fussy four-year-old or the calm way in which she deals with a household emergency.
- Ask for acknowledgment. Whoever told you that acknowledgment that you have to ask for "doesn't count" was wrong. There are lots of reasons why your siblings may fail to acknowledge your consideration and generosity, including forgetting, not knowing what to say, and being preoccupied with their own concerns. This does not mean that they do not appreciate what you have done or that their acknowledgment, when it finally comes, is insincere.

Chapter 3

Know Yourself: The Value of Self-Awareness

Sometimes, inevitably, siblings will fail to acknowledge the things you have done for them and the times you have thought about them, been considerate of their feelings, and gone out of your way for them. At other times, again inevitably, your siblings will fail to appreciate the difficulties in your life—the challenges you face, the struggles you have been through, the mountains you have climbed to get where you are. The acknowledgment that you hope for and deserve will not always materialize.

Become Self-Aware

In these situations, learning to acknowledge your own contributions to others is the best preventive measure to take to avoid disappointment and resentment.

Josephine's Story: "It's Not Fair!"

Josephine made it a point to attend all the important events—big and small—in her brother's and sister's lives and those of their children. Yet her brother and sister rarely reciprocated, and Josephine couldn't understand why. Worst of all, they didn't acknowledge that they were unable to place as high a priority on her family's celebrations as she did on theirs.

Josephine's reactions ran the gamut, from surprise and disappointment, through sadness, to anger and resentment. Underlying all these emotions were two beliefs: she was a fool to go out of her way to be present at those other events and celebrations, and her siblings were selfish and uncaring. As she told me, "I'm simply not going to go out of my way again for any of them. The next time they're celebrating something, I'll say what they always say to me: 'Sorry, it doesn't seem to be in the cards.' Maybe I won't even bother to reply at all."

Examine Your Motives

Josephine's reactions are not unusual. When the hoped-for acknowledgment from a sibling never arrives, many people become angry because of the unfairness, and question their own motives. But trying to decide whether you did the right thing based on how your sibling responds is always a mistake. It is far better to learn to evaluate the efforts *you* make to show caring and kindness to your sibling. Then you can give yourself credit for what you have done, rather than waiting around for your brother or sister to appreciate you.

Josephine came to this understanding after we had talked together. This enabled her to make a new plan for the future. "I'm still disappointed in them," she told me during one of our sessions, "and I'm still angry, too." But seeing family is fun for me, and seeing the kids celebrate their special moments is fun, too. I thought I was doing it to please my brothers and sisters, but it's just as much to please myself—and the kids. I think it's nice for kids to have uncles and aunts who show that they're proud of them.

"I don't understand why my brothers and sisters don't enjoy celebrating with us as much as I enjoy celebrating with them, but I figure it's their loss. If I decided to get even by not going to my nephew's high school graduation, I'd regret it. So

I guess what it comes down to is this: I wish they cared more. I wish they were different. They're not, and there's nothing I can do about it. But I don't want to let myself become more like them just because I'm hurt, even though I feel like it sometimes."

In other words, the acknowledgment Josephine sought from her siblings ultimately came from inside herself instead.

There are many other situations in which giving yourself the acknowledgment you desire from others helps your relationship with your sibling.

Paula's Story: "What's Wrong with Me?"

Paula was one of those organized people who began shopping for Christmas gifts for her family and friends in August. She prided herself on being able to find the perfect gift for each person on her list, especially for her older sister Amelia. She knew that Amelia loved crafts and so looked hard for things that would surprise and delight her. One year she bought her a handmade quilt, another year a sweater knitted by Inuit natives from musk ox wool.

One summer, visiting her sister, Paula went looking for a lightbulb in a large closet only to accidentally discover several gifts from years past still neatly nestled in their original packages. When she confronted Amelia about this, Amelia said, "The gifts were lovely; I'm just keeping them there until I can use them." Paula felt terrible, assuming that Amelia had not liked the gifts at all and was just being polite.

Paula, a warm and sensitive person, wasn't angry with Amelia, but was angry and disappointed with herself. She was also sad and full of self-blame. My goal, I told Paula, was to help her use this experience to learn to decide for herself whether she had done the right thing without relying on what somebody else—her sister, in this case—might think or say.

We began by reviewing Paula's shopping habits. She remembered how much time and thought she had put into choosing each gift as well as how she had spent unselfishly in the hope of bringing pleasure to her sister. Then I asked Paula if she thought it made more sense for her to judge herself and her gift giving by her sister's response, or by weighing her own thoughtfulness and generosity. Paula agreed that the latter made sense, and although she still felt sadness at her sister's apparent lack of appreciation, she no longer felt that her self-esteem had been undermined.

Paula is far from being alone in evaluating her own actions based on whether they produce the desired response in another person. Interpersonal sensitivity is a great asset that can also be a burden. People who are thoughtful about themselves and their most intimate relationships—people who read books like this one—are much more likely to be aware of the effect they have on others and to show compassion and consideration for others. There can be no question that the world would be a better place if more people were like this. Based on two decades of experience in working with families with young children, I know that children benefit enormously when their parents possess this kind of sensitivity. People who aren't naturally particularly sensitive to other people's feelings and needs, who don't readily notice how their words and deeds affect other people, need help in developing these skills.

It's possible, however, to take a good thing too far. If, like Paula, you tend to assume responsibility for everything that goes wrong between you and your siblings, and even some things that don't really go wrong but just appear to do so, your problem lies in the opposite direction. Far from needing to increase your capacity for empathy and interpersonal sensitivity, you need to learn to trust yourself and to question your sibling a bit more. The previous chapter gave you some techniques to increase your awareness of your sibling's positive intentions, whether or not those intentions always result in positive outcomes. It's just as important to be fully aware of your own positive intentions and to credit yourself for your attempts to do the right thing.

If you find yourself in the same situation as Jennifer or Paula, remember what they learned:

- You, not your sibling, are in charge of how you feel about what you do.
- You, not your sibling, will decide if you did the right thing.
- You, not your sibling, will decide if you acted with consideration or with narrow self-interest.

Acknowledge "Difficult" Feelings

Jealousy, envy, resentment, and shame are difficult but human emotions that won't go away no matter how much we want them to. They can undo many otherwise positive and cooperative relationships. And yet they are hardwired within us, part of the human fabric. Acknowledging these feelings is often the first step toward clearing the air with your sibling. For if they are not acknowledged, they can easily turn into anger, disdain, and rejection.

Mary's Story: "I Wish I Had As Much As You"

Mary was forever complaining about how materialistic her sister was, how she spent money on cars, vacations, and jewelry. So preoccupied was she with this that she didn't stop to ask herself the central question: "Why does this bother me so much?" Even when I asked the question quite directly, Mary tried to avoid answering it: "Why does it bother me? It would bother anybody! Wouldn't it bother you?"

The answer was not complicated. Mary wished that she herself had more money. Once she was able to tolerate facing this truth, she realized that there was nothing to be gained by being angry with her sister. She no longer acted as if her sister's success somehow diminished what she, Mary, had accomplished. She realized that what she had been doing was partly out of embarrassment and shame. She had not allowed herself to fully realize that she wanted to be able to spend money and buy things as her sister did and had instead turned those feelings into anger with Mary.

This was totally unfair, since Mary's sister hadn't taken anything from her. Mary also realized that one of the things that had been sustaining her envy was paradoxical. The more shame she felt about being so envious, the more she struggled to deny it, and the more anger she felt toward her sister. The more that she was able to accept her envy, and her very understandable wish for greater wealth, the more her anger diminished. When Mary was able to accept that it was quite natural and normal to want things that she saw her sister enjoying, she felt a great burden lift from her.

Remember, it's easy to justify your feelings of resentment and envy toward siblings. The challenge is to find ways to overcome these feelings, through self-acceptance, as Mary did.

If you find yourself in Mary's shoes, ask yourself:

- What do I gain from harboring these feelings toward my sibling?
- What might I gain if I let them go?

Feelings Are Natural, But Not Necessarily Infallible

Mary's strength was in acknowledging her true feelings and then moving on. Many people, however, get stuck after the acknowledgment—and that can lead to problems.

Though evolutionary psychologists believe that jealousy, aggression, and other "difficult" emotions are part of our genetic heritage and that we should simply accept them, I maintain that if we are to be fully human we must overcome some feelings that may appear to be natural. After all, some species closely related to us commit rape and infanticide. Are we to conclude that these "natural" behaviors are also acceptable?

Similarly, some people believe that "spontaneous" expressions of feelings are more "real" than less immediate expressions. But people who feel this way often have a very difficult time improving their relationships with their siblings, as well as with other people in their lives. There's no reason to assume that what we say in the heat of the moment is how we really feel. It's just how we feel at that moment.

Take Mike, for example. He showed his brother Ed a book about financial planning that he'd just bought. "I'll lend it to you when I'm done with it, if you want," Mike said.

"You think I don't invest my money well?" Ed said angrily. "I already know everything in that book; I've been doing it for years."

Mike hadn't expected this reaction from his brother, and he was sorely tempted to respond angrily in kind. Instead, he paused long enough to take a few deep breaths and then asked, "Does it bother you that I was trying to share something with you that I found useful?"

This question, voicing his confusion, enabled the brothers to have a conversation about their pattern of interaction. Notice, though, that if Mike had acted on his first, supposedly "true" feeling—anger—nothing good would have ensued. It was only because he took a moment to calm himself and experience his other feelings, including confusion, that the conversation took a productive turn.

Can you honestly say that Mike's anger was "truer" than his confusion? To my way of thinking, just because one feelings precedes another doesn't make it any truer.

Yet the myth persists that feelings of the moment are more genuine and truthful than more measured responses. This is part of a larger pattern of the belief that feelings in general can't be questioned. Many people come into my office and say things like:

- I'm just saying how I really feel.
- I can't change how I feel.
- If I said anything else, I'd be lying.
- I don't want to be a phony.

In fact, some psychologists, psychiatrists, and social workers believe that feelings are the most important factor in all close relationships, and that feelings are inviolate and not open to question. They believe that if their patients feel anger or envy, and try to act as if they didn't, they would be fooling themselves and no good would come of it.

They also believe that their feelings about a person, a relationship, or an event are somehow caused by that person, relationship, or event. And since these feelings are automatic and inevitable consequences, they can't be legitimately challenged or questioned. They believe that their feelings are a part of them, much as their hair color is red or brown. Anyone who suggests that they need not feel as they do is typically described as "discounting" their feelings, or perhaps as trying to control them. The typical response, often expressed with incredulity, to anyone who suggests that their feelings may not be absolutely called for, or that other people might not feel the same way, is, "Are you saying that my feelings aren't legitimate?"

Underlying this assumption is the belief that feelings occupy a special place in life, that they are true in the way that Newton's law, of physics are true. To question feelings, or to wonder if a situation really requires so much anger, for example, is tantamount to asking if the apple is justified in falling from the tree.

But is this really true? Are feelings inviolate? Are they always necessary by-products of events, people, and relationships? If so, they are completely different from our thoughts, which everybody recognizes as often erroneous. If we can make errors in writing down a phone number, scheduling an appointment, or remembering a name, why, in the same way, why can't our feelings sometimes be mistaken?

The answer is that they can be, and often are.

There is nothing about experiencing an emotion that ensures that your interpretation of its cause will be accurate. This is more true for some emotions than others, and is especially true for anger and fear. For one thing, anger and fear both occur in conjunction with elevated levels of adrenaline, the body's "fight or flight" hormone. High levels of adrenaline occur when people are very frightened or extremely angry; when the body is preparing to run away or quite literally to fight. The physical sensations are the same: sweaty palms, elevated blood pressure and heart rate, feelings of tightness in the chest and abdomen. The accompanying thoughts are different; the causes are different; the meanings are different.

This is where those difficult feelings come in. You may believe that your sister's flashy lifestyle makes you envious. The truth is that it is your own thoughts that upset you and make you envious. Recognizing this will not immediately change how you feel. What it will do is give you a way to begin to examine the roots of your upsetting feelings about your sister or brother and a way to begin to gain control over your feelings.

Start by analyzing what you are thinking as you begin to get upset. For many people, the thoughts that accompany jealousy and envy run like this:

55

- My sister is beautiful/engaged/rich/has a great apartment and I'm not and/or I don't.
- That is horribly unfair and I can't bear it.
- If I don't get engaged, a big apartment, a fabulous job, I'll just die.
- This is the most horrible thing that could happen.
- I hate her!

When you have thoughts like these, ask yourself:

- Are these thoughts rational?
- Do I really believe them?

Or is this closer to what you really believe: "I wish I had some of the things my sister has. I think I would be happier. I would really prefer to be beautiful/engaged/have a great apartment."

If you analyze your thoughts in this way, you'll find that what you really believe is, "I'd prefer it if things were different," not "This is the end of the world."

There are other instances in which focusing on feelings can lead you and your sibling astray.

Focus on Fairness, Not Feelings

When we focus on feelings, to the exclusion of everything else, we may conclude that we can judge whether or not we did the right thing by how our sibling feels about it. The problem with this, however, is that many factors other than what you do or don't do may be affecting how your sibling feels.

For example, when Rachel's sister Debbie told her that she would not be able to come to Rachel's only child's bar mitzvah because of a work conflict, Rachel was stunned. She reminded Debbie that it was a once-in-a-lifetime event and that theirs was a small family. She also made it very clear how much it would mean to her if Debbie could be there.

56

Debbie protested. "You're trying to lay a guilt trip on me," she said. Rachel had anticipated this reaction and was clear in herself that her intention was not to make Debbie feel guilty but to let her know how much her presence would contribute to the special day. Because she had already thought it through, she was able to tell Debbie, "I'm sorry if it seems that I'm trying to make you feel guilty. I'm not. I just want you to know how important this is to me."

A good way to inoculate yourself against reacting too strongly to a sibling's emotional reaction, as Rachel did, is to learn to ask yourself these questions:

- Did I carefully think about how what I did or said would affect my sibling?
- Did I intend to be considerate? to be caring? to be helpful?
- Did I intentionally do anything that would be hurtful?
- Did I do or say anything that I would not want my brother or sister to do or say to me?

If your answers to these questions indicate genuine caring, then you should give yourself credit for being exceptionally considerate and caring, regardless of how your sibling reacts.

Remember, there is a huge difference between doing the right thing and ensuring the result that you want. All too often, good intentions can lead to bad results. Focus your attention on the former.

Revisiting the Past with Awareness

You can bring this same sense of self-awareness to bear when you try to evaluate how your childhood feelings, experiences, and memories color your present relationships with your siblings.

Joanne, for example, still thought of her sister as the bossy big sister she had been twenty years earlier. It wasn't only that Joanne remembered her sister as having been bossy; she experienced her as being bossy today as well. No matter how her older sister acted in the present, Joanne perceived her through the lens of the past, through a twenty-year-old lens. When her sister asked her where she got her hair cut, Joanne immediately prepared for the put-down—only it never came.

In fact, Joanne spent so much of her time interacting with her sister while anticipating the negative that she was unable to see or appreciate the positives. Though she was very aware of how much she had changed since childhood, she was blind to her sister's changes. In her eyes, her sister was as bossy and mean as she'd been twenty years ago.

Perhaps your childhood memories are influencing your reactions to your siblings today, clouding and distorting your perceptions. If you want to find a new way to relate to your brother or sister, if you want to try to initiate new and healthier patterns of interaction with them, consider how you can become more aware of the ways in which these old experiences live today. Here is an exercise that has helped many people I've worked with.

❖   ❖   ❖

An Exercise to Increase Self-Awareness

Whenever an encounter with your brother or sister leads you to experience a strong negative feeling, whether anger, frustration, irritation, sadness, disappointment, jealousy, tension, anxiety, or some other difficult feeling, take a few minutes to ask yourself if the feeling is familiar. Is it a feeling you've had before? Is it a feeling you had as a child, and still have? If so, try to remember one of the first times you felt that way. Try to recall what was happening, who was there, and the thoughts you had that accompanied the unpleasant feeling.

Having identified a possible historical connection for your feeling, ask yourself if you are truly upset about your current experience or if you are, rather, upset once again about the earlier situation. Was the new event merely a trigger that led you to reexperience that earlier unpleasant time? This sort of triggering and reexperiencing happens all the time. In its more pleasant and benign form, it occurs when a mild spring day brings back memories of a carefree childhood. In its most negative, extreme form, it is known as posttraumatic stress disorder and occurs among victims of war and other violence as well as others who have experienced extreme trauma.

The best thing that you can do to separate that past unpleasant event and your present circumstance is to verbalize, to yourself or to someone else, all the differences between the earlier event and the current one. Do this as many times as it takes to make the differences real, vivid, and concrete.

- Remind yourself of all the ways in which the exchange you just had with your brother is different from those you had with him when you were eight and he was twelve.
- Remember that he may have been able to bring you to tears then, but that now you can defend yourself verbally.
- Remember that it may have seemed that your self-esteem depended on his approval then, but now it does not.

❖   ❖   ❖

❖ ❖ ❖

HOW TO HANDLE BLAME

Of all the emotions, guilt is one of the most unpleasant. Most of us go to great lengths to avoid feeling guilty. One of the easiest, and so the most tempting ways to escape feelings of guilt is by pinning the responsibility for whatever caused the feeling on another person—your brother, for example. In other words, a good way to avoid guilt is to blame someone else: "It's not my fault that I lost my temper, screamed, and told my brother he had his head screwed on backward—it's his fault for being so damn stubborn and rigid."

When Jerri asked her sister Linda if they could have a heart-to heart talk to improve their relationship, Linda was nervous but was very pleased as well. But as it turned out, Jerri used this frank and open conversation as an opportunity to talk about how three or four difficult events during their childhood continued to plague her today. Linda had to fight the urge to say, "Get over it!," or, alternatively, "Are you trying to tell me that something that I did when you were seven and I was ten has shaped your whole life, and that it is my fault that we do not have a better relationship?"

To Linda's credit, she did not say either of these things, but she certainly would have been entitled to. After all, her sister had pretty clearly implied just that, that it was Linda's fault that things had not been different twenty or twenty-five years earlier.

Unfortunately, Jerri had not learned to frame her concerns in the kind of language that facilitates dialogue. By blaming Linda, Jerri nearly squandered a wonderful opportunity to get their relationship back on track.

Imagine how much more smoothly things would have gone for Jerri and how much more progress would have been made if she had said, "You know, I have this terrible problem in that I can't seem to get over the past. I know it's childish in some ways, but I'm really stuck. Would it be all right with you if at those times when I'm aware that I'm distorting what you are saying, if I tell you and sort of do a reality check? You know, like if I said, 'Linda this is one of those times that I keep feeling that you're putting me down, but I'm not sure. What did you mean by what you just said?'"

Fortunately, Linda had learned how to respond in a way that allows conversations to continue, and had practiced it during some of our meetings. When Jerri confronted her, she responded with concern rather than defensiveness. "Jerri, it sounds like you're still hurting. I don't remember our childhood as well as you do, but I'm sorry if I upset you. What can I do to make it up to you?" As Linda related it to me later, Jerri had been waiting for years to be heard. It was all that was needed to begin a process of healing.

If you realize that you have an inaccurate and decades-old image of your brother, it is up to you to change it. He can hardly go back and be different as a child, can he?

Instead of blaming, an old game that nobody can win, adopt a solution-oriented perspective. If you can't get all that old stuff out of your head, and if you find it nearly irresistible to tell your brother about it at every opportunity, something is seriously amiss. What is amiss is most probably that you feel the need for acknowledgment that you are trying to get your mind clear and to learn to live in the present.

If this rings true for you, try the direct approach: ask your brother to acknowledge your efforts. If such a request feels awkward, say so. "You know, I feel a little foolish saying this, but I wanted you to know that I've been trying really hard to keep in mind that all those things I remember from so long ago, and blame you for, were not your fault any more than having blue eyes was. I've been trying to see you as you truly are. It would mean a lot to me to know that you can tell I'm trying and that you can see my efforts, I mean, if you *can* see them."

Wordy, sure. Awkward, sure. But it gets the point across and is a lot more likely to generate the sort of response you hope for rather than yet more blame.

When you decide that the time is right to make a move toward a better relationship with your sibling, avoid blaming statements—they lead nowhere. Instead, look first to yourself and how you can change so that the relationship will improve.

❖   ❖   ❖

Sometimes Silence Is Golden

You've just read a great deal of advice about how understanding yourself can help you figure out what to say and when to say it. But there are also times when self-awareness can lead you to say nothing.

Hank, who had not had the best of luck with women, had been dating Allison for eight months before he introduced her to anyone in his family. His sister Marianne, who had felt very happy that Hank had finally found someone with whom he clicked, felt guilty that she did not really like Allison. Though Allison was very pleasant, Marianne couldn't warm up to her. In fact, with time, she liked the girl less instead of more. She couldn't shake the feeling that there was something untrustworthy about her. She seriously considered telling her brother just what she thought of his girlfriend, not to hurt him, but to advise him to be cautious about the relationship.

Marianne thought about her options for a very long time. After considering the possible benefits to Hank and to her relationship with him, as well as the possible harm that might come from speaking her mind—that Hank would dismiss her or, worse, become angry with her—she decided to say nothing.

As it turned out, Marianne's decision was the right one. Hank and Allison broke up some months later. Hank then admitted to his sister that he'd always had his doubts about Allison though he had tried to deny them. When Marianne told him of her reservations, and that she had debated speaking her mind, Hank thanked her for her concern and said, "I'm glad you kept out of it. I wouldn't have believed you anyway."

Action Steps for Positive Self-Awareness

For those times that a brother or a sister quite directly tells you that you are to blame for an awkward situation, or that you "made" him or her feel or act a certain way, remember:

- Nobody can control anybody else's behavior.
- You are the best judge of your own intentions. Patty, the woman you met in the introductory chapter, whose sister Lucy suddenly changed her mind about a shared vacation, found that she felt much better about what she had done to reach out to her sister after she looked to herself for both evaluation and acknowledgment.
- When you have tried to do the right thing and nobody recognized it, be sure to recognize it yourself.
- When your brother or sister "explains" why you shouldn't feel as you do, remember to credit your own experience as much as you do theirs.
- If you find yourself feeling a bit depressed when your brother or sister talks with you about how you can improve your relationship, to uncover covert blame, think carefully about what he or she is saying. If the blame is there, trust your own assessment of your behavior.

PART 2

Strategies for Healing Sibling Relationships

Chapter 4

How to Talk—and Listen to—Your Sibling

Talking and listening—there are few activities we take more for granted than these. Yet effective communication requires a number of skills:

- knowing how to use language to communicate
- learning to appreciate how your sibling uses language
- learning to listen
- appreciating your sibling's strengths and weaknesses as a communicator
- and, above all, appreciating your own strengths and weaknesses as a communicator

It is often said that two people are in conflict because "they are not communicating"; the truth is always more complex and subtler than that. People are always communicating something, even when they are not talking. The problem is that the two people involved frequently have very different ideas about what is being communicated.

Understanding Communication Styles

Good communication centers on learning about your sibling and what your sibling has to say, putting your own thoughts and feelings into words, and exchanging information. If people were without flaws, we would all have perfect hearing, perfect vision, and perfect recall of everything we see or hear, perfect comprehension of everything anyone says to us as well as of everything we observe, a perfect ability to choose exactly the right word from a limitless vocabulary, and a perfect ability to synthesize all this different information. But, since none of us has the gift of a perfect nervous system, nobody can do this. In a sense, everybody has a learning disability.

Some people have the advantage of knowing what their learning disabilities are. These lucky few have learned, perhaps as a result of experiences in school or at work, about the kinds of learning situations and tasks that come less than naturally to them. They may have discovered that they experience difficulty in paying careful attention to what someone is saying if there are any distractions in the environment, or that they easily forget details, or that they have trouble putting their feelings into words, or that they must struggle to sense what another person may be feeling or is likely to feel in a given situation. For the rest of us, discovering our learning strengths and weaknesses is a gradual process involving a lot of trial and error. The trials (and the errors) are worth it because the more you know about your strengths and weaknesses as listeners and speakers, the more you will be able to do to facilitate smoother, more informative, more comfortable, and less conflicted communication between you and your siblings.

Stephanie's Story: "But That's Not What I Meant!"

Stephanie Andrews was talking on the telephone with her older brother Jack about developments in his business when her three-year-old daughter, Stacie, began crying because she had dropped her Popsicle. Stephanie put the phone down for a moment to comfort her. When she came back to the phone, Jack said, "Do you realize that whenever we talk on the phone you are always interrupting me to do something else?" Stephanie said that she hadn't realized it. She had not meant to be rude and she was sorry if it had seemed that way. Jack, unable to accept his sister's apology, couldn't let his anger go. "It's not really a matter of being rude," he said. "I think it's more of an ethical issue."

Stephanie, an attorney, had recently been appointed to the local bar association's ethics committee. Hearing her brother, she felt her adrenaline begin to flow and her blood pressure rise. In a flash, she could see that what had happened so many times before was about to happen again. How many times had her brother said something that she took as demeaning or sarcastic? How many times had she reacted rapidly, applying her quick wit and considerable verbal facility in a way that felt defensive to her, but felt aggressive and insulting to Jack? She knew that she could easily hurt Jack, who felt inadequate because he had not finished college, by criticizing his choice of words and by challenging him to define the meaning of the word "ethics." How many times had she reacted with ferocity to one of her brother's statements, sparking a firestorm that took months to die down?

This was just the sort of heated exchange that had prompted Stephanie to ask me for help. We'd talked a great deal about why she and her brother got into so many really nasty arguments when she cared about him deeply and knew that he cared about her as well. Over time, she'd realized that though careful language was important to her, professionally and personally, it was far less important to Jack—who was a successful landscape artist and watercolorist. She also realized that her brother was prone to the Cheshire cat's approach to semantics ("A word means what I say it means").

Thanks to this new understanding, Stephanie didn't react defensively or impulsively when her brother used the word "ethics" in what she considered a careless way. Instead, she took a moment to reflect on her brother's style of communicating. She realized that Jack didn't mean to impugn her ethics; he simply couldn't find the right words to express his hurt feelings.

Had she not figured this out, she could easily have been offended and gotten embroiled in a nasty argument and hurt feelings. Instead, Stephanie ignored his comment and returned the conversation to its original intent: "And have you had luck in finding that new assistant you were looking for?" she asked her brother.

Embrace Your Differences

Many communication difficulties arise when we forget that our particular strengths may not be those of our siblings. Like Stephanie, you may be very comfortable using language to communicate your feelings, and exquisitely tuned in to how other people use language as well. Someone like Jack, on the other hand, is less interested in (and less comfortable with) the subtleties of language. What mattered to him weren't dictionary definitions but how he felt using language. He was more sensitive to the subtleties of light, space, and pattern than to fine distinctions between written or spoken words.

Shirley and her brother Andy have a different sort of communication problem. Shirley lives for details and always relates a story one step at a time, often including verbatim quotations from the people involved in a way that would make any trial attorney proud. Her brother Andy likes to get right to the bottom line; the process is much less important to him than the product. Predictably, Andy becomes impatient with Shirley's stories and interrupts her, often saying, "Would you get to the point?! I'm beginning to lose you here!" Shirley is frustrated by this, because for her it is impossible to fully appreciate the significance of "the point" without knowing the steps that led up to it. So she asks questions, lots of questions. This frustrates Andy, who wants to convey the big picture quickly, without a lot of "wasted time." The solution I was able to help them arrive at—one that may help you, too—was to agree to remind each other of their different styles so that each could try to accommodate the other a bit.

If you assume that your brother's or your sister's mind works just as yours does, the differences can also lead to misunderstandings. If you are the sort of person who can be involved in three conversations at once and who never forgets a voice, it will take some effort to appreciate that not everyone's mind works this way. If you have never been lost, can remember where every piece of furniture was in your parent's living room twenty years ago, and can easily visualize the route from Albany to Brattleboro, you will have to work hard to understand why your sister needs you to repeat directions three times and then has to write them down. These preferred ways of taking in new information apply to all areas of life: learning about the news of the day, getting or giving directions, learning about the progress of a business or a professional project. They also apply to the ways in which we are most comfortable expressing our personal thoughts, feelings, aspirations, and needs to those we are closest to.

These differences can derail your sibling relationship if you overlook them—or they can enrich your conversations and your relationship.

❖ ❖ ❖

IDENTIFYING YOUR COMMUNICATION STYLE

The following questions can help you identify some of your preferred ways of adding to your information about the world and other people and, by extension, the way in which you probably most naturally share information with others:

- When you are learning to use a VCR, computer, or camera, do you rely more on the diagrams or the written instructions?
- When you give someone directions, are you more likely to draw a map or write out turn-by-turn directions?
- Which are you more likely to remember, what you saw at a place you visited or what someone said to you when you were there?
- If you had to choose, would you look at pictures of an event or read about it?
- When you read a newspaper or magazine article that includes charts, graphs, and diagrams, do you skip the text and study the images, skip the images and read the text, or do both?
- Do you frequently make drawings to illustrate something you want to say?
- Do you like to emphasize a point by using visual analogies such as "It's like a house crashing down?"
- Do you like to emphasize a point by using language based analogies such as, it's like Henry said, "we band of brothers, we lucky few"?
- Does it drive you crazy when someone is speaking to you while you are on the phone with another person or does it seem like the most natural thing in the world?

Your answers will reflect what kind of information you like to receive from other people and what kind you are most inclined to give to them. The purpose of this informal assessment is not to try to change who you are, but to be more aware of it.

Now, think about a brother or a sister with whom communication has been difficult. Go back through the list of questions and answer them as you think your brother or your sister would. Are their responses similar to yours? If not, one of your difficulties may be that you are speaking the same language, but in very different ways.

Once you have identified the differences in how you and your siblings are most at home in communicating the most important thing is to remember that these differences exist. As you have read in earlier chapters, it is always better to try to figure out what you can do to improve your relationships with your siblings rather than blaming them or trying to get them to change. This is especially true of communication difficulties. Try to adjust your communication style to suit the brother or sister with whom you are talking. If you are one of those people who truly can focus on a conversation (either face-to-face or on the telephone) while listening to the radio or writing a grocery list, but you know that this drives your brother or your sister crazy, don't force them to do this.

❖   ❖   ❖

Talking to Your Sibling

When it comes to what you actually say to your sibling, there are three guidelines I urge you to remember:

- Think of your sibling's reality, not your own.
- Don't be sarcastic.
- Think before you speak.

See Your Siblings for Who They Are

It's completely natural to relate to others, especially to our brothers and sisters, at least partly through our own experiences. It is just as natural to assume that your sibling means the same thing when he says something that you would if you said it. Unfortunately, these natural tendencies often lead to misperception, miscommunication, and misunderstanding. Just think about what would have happened if Stephanie seriously thought that her brother Jack was accusing her of being unethical, rather than saying that she had hurt his feelings. This is yet another reason to be sure to think about what your brother or your sister means by any remark that distresses or upsets you. When you can do this, you may find that the upset is totally unnecessary!

When we project our own needs and experiences onto our siblings so much that we fail to see them clearly, problems are inevitable. Imagine a movie of your early life playing inside your head in an endless loop. Now imagine that this movie is being projected outside you, onto a movie screen covering your siblings' faces and bodies. Imagine that you are unable to see what your siblings are doing, unable to hear what they are saying, unable to see facial expressions or appreciate how they are feeling, all because what would otherwise be a clear view of them is blocked by the projected movie. Finally, imagine that you respond to the projected movie images and sounds rather than to the real people who are your brothers and your sisters.

You would inevitably be defensive when you should instead be seeking clarification, angry when you should be sympathetic, critical when you should be supportive, blaming when you should be praising, amused when you should be stern, and oblivious when you should be delighted. This is what happens when you project your real or imagined self onto a brother or a sister and then react to that projected-upon sibling rather than to the real person. Solving this problem requires real work.

Exercise:

• The next time you are about to say something negative to your brother or your sister, whether it is critical or complaining, ask yourself if you are truly reacting to what you heard or saw or to something in yourself, a filter through which you interpreted what you heard or saw.

Find a Substitute for Sarcasm

Lady Astor is reported to have remarked to Sir Winston Churchill at a dinner party, "Sir, if you were my husband, I should put poison in your tea."

According to the story, Sir Winston replied: "Madam, if I were your husband, I should drink it."

This sort of exchange of put-downs, whether or not it ever actually occurred, is entertaining to read about. It is not, however, an ideal model for improving or healing an injured relationship. *If you want to communicate well, never be sarcastic: it kills communication.*

Thinly veiled mockery, gratuitous put-downs, sarcasm, and other forms of one-upmanship all have the same motivation—to make the speaker feel superior to his target. They also have the same effect: each creates hurt and distance between people.

I'm aware that some people may read this and think, "Come on, lighten up! A joke is just a joke." Is sarcasm a joke, though? Is it humor? What is sarcasm anyway? *Webster's Ninth New Collegiate Dictionary* defines sarcasm as "a sharp and often satirical or ironic utterance designed to cut or give pain," and notes that it is derived from French, Latin, and

Greek words that originally meant "to tear flesh, to bite the lips in rage, to sneer." Sarcasm has only one purpose: to inflict a wound. It neither opens a dialogue nor fosters communication. All it does is hurt feelings and build walls of resentment. Make a solemn vow to yourself to give up these modes of communication altogether. If you can't do that, at least vow not to use them with close relatives.

Learn to Stop Yourself

If you pick up only one new idea from this chapter, it should be this: think carefully about how what you are about to say or do will affect the present moment between you and your sibling and how it may affect every moment to come as well. Just because you can think of a quick retort to every remark doesn't mean that you should deliver it.

Stephanie was able to sidestep a fight with her brother by virtue of what she *didn't* say. She kept her snappy comebacks to herself, and the conversation continued without incident. That doesn't mean that she won't ever speak to Jack about his careless use of words. She just realized that his touchiness was an issue for another time.

And she was able to do this because she took a moment to consider the consequences of her saying something caustic in response to him. A fight would have ensued, which would have colored their relationship for an indefinite period of time, leaving them with the badly bruised feelings that often resulted from misunderstandings between the two of them.

Ultimately, what was most valuable in this exchange was not anything that Stephanie said, but her willingness and ability to refrain from saying any of the many defensive, insulting, and potentially damaging things that came into her mind.

Exercise

- Before responding to your sibling, ask yourself if what you are about to say will help your brother or your sister. Is it likely to contribute to your relationship in a positive way? Or is it just a way for you to vent?

I do not mean to imply that it is never productive to complain about a sibling's behavior or that anger is always counterproductive; neither of these statements is defensible. But there is a difference between an angry complaint that is based in reality and provides a possibility of positive change and a cathartic outpouring that does nothing but create bad feelings. One involves a clearing of the air so that you and your brother can get to work and improve things. The other is a flame that produces heat without light.

How to Complain

So far, this chapter has focused on how to tame potential conflicts before they erupt. I have encouraged you to think carefully and to question your own perceptions and interpretations before saying anything that might make things worse between you and your sibling. But are there no times when a person can have a legitimate complaint? Does everything between siblings have to be lovely all the time, with never a disagreement or a conflict?

Naturally, this isn't realistic. But there are some guidelines to voicing a complaint that help guarantee satisfaction.

- *Be like Sergeant Joe Friday.* When you have a complaint, stick to the facts. The more objective you can be, the better.
- *Avoid attributions.* Since you can't really be sure why your sibling did or said something, don't attribute meaning to his behavior. If he never asks how your

children are doing in school, but always tells you about his children's accomplishments, it may be because he isn't interested, but it may also be because he is preoccupied about his kids, maybe even anxious about them.

- *Don't ask questions when you're not interested in the answer.* There are times when you may want to know why your sister hasn't called or visited your mother in two months, but there are probably more times when you really just want to say: "I'd like you to go see Mom this week."
- *Don't wait too long.* When you realize that you are unhappy about something that a sibling has said or done (or perhaps failed to say or do), look for a quick opportunity to sort things out. Resentments build quickly and just as quickly cause secondary problems to develop from what may originally have been a simple one.
- *When uncertain about what to say, be honest.* If you must talk to your brother about an awkward subject, or if you just feel awkward bringing up a past disagreement, there's nothing wrong with saying, "I feel really awkward about this, but . . ."

Being Kind and Appreciative Helps

Beyond learning how to criticize constructively, look for opportunities to express appreciation and support. Positive spontaneous comments go a long way toward keeping siblings close.

Liz, spent a long weekend with her husband Ralph's sister Amelia. After witnessing one unpleasant encounter after another between Ralph and Amelia, Liz spontaneously called her own brother Jim, who had recently moved two hundred and fifty miles away. He was not in, so she left a message on his answering machine, saying, "Hi, I'm here with Ralph and Amelia. Without going into a lot of unnecessary detail, I just wanted to say that I'm really glad that you're my brother." Jim called back later in the week and also left a message in which he said, "Got your message. Sounds great! I can't wait to hear more!"

Liz was pleased and amused. She made a joke to her husband about her brother's unusual sense of humor and the implication that he wanted to hear more about what a great brother he was. Liz's decision to call had several benefits: Jim felt acknowledged for being "a good brother," and Liz benefited from the good feeling she got from his reaction.

All these techniques will help you in conversation with your sibling. But talking is only one half of the equation: listening is the important other half.

The Art of Listening to Your Sibling

Artists say that the essence of learning to draw or paint is learning to see. In the same way, the essence of learning to communicate is learning to listen.

Listening carefully can go a long way toward solving the problem of unwittingly projecting your life and life experiences onto your sibling. Few things make people as angry as when they feel as if others are not listening to them. On the other hand, those people who do feel that they are being heard often feel tremendous pleasure and gratification—they appreciate the fact that someone made the effort to listen.

This is not nearly as easy as it sounds. Sherlock Holmes told his friend, "My dear Watson, you see, but you do not observe." All too often, we hear what our brothers and sisters say, but we do not understand or appreciate the significance of what we hear because our ability to appreciate a sibling's perspective is blocked. So-called active listening skills, such as repeating what your sibling has just said, are helpful but are not enough. What is needed is a genuine commitment to understanding.

You can achieve this by realizing that conversations have two components: what is actually said, which we call the content; and the tone of the conversation, or how the content is said, which we call process.

Focus on the Content of Conversations by Asking Questions

Even the most active listeners can't correctly interpret every remark someone else makes. *So part of being a good listener is learning to ask the right questions.* Ask them with real interest, as someone who is really trying to understand. Remember that when your brother or sister says something, it does not necessarily mean what it would if you said it. This alone is guaranteed to reduce misunderstandings and conflicts.

Questions that help understanding

Make sure that you have truly heard the words that your sibling has uttered. You can get away with missing a word or so at a cocktail party, or when bantering, but if the topic is important, make sure you have heard every word. Don't be afraid of asking your brother or your sister to repeat something if that's what it takes to understand what was said.

Questions that impede understanding

There are few things more irritating than hearing someone say, "I hear where you're coming from," when you know he does not understand or care where you are coming from at all. Before you tell your brother or your sister that you know where they are coming from, try to be sure that you really do understand. The single best question to ask whenever a discussion begins to get sticky is, "What do you mean?" The single best statement at similar times is, "I don't understand." Do not ask or say these things sarcastically.

These strategies sound straightforward, but they are sometimes hard to put into practice. That's because many conversations begin with the focus on content, but veer off, midstream, into discussions of process.

Wanda's Story: "What do you mean"?

Wanda invited her sister Jennifer and her family to come to her home for Thanksgiving, and Jennifer naturally asked if she could bring something. When Wanda suggested that it would be nice to have a pumpkin pie, Jennifer responded, "I have a problem with your asking me to do that."

Wanda's first reaction was puzzlement. She wasn't sure if Jennifer was responding to something in Wanda's tone of voice when she suggested that Jennifer make the pie, or if Jennifer was reconsidering her offer.

At this moment, their conversation was on the verge of detouring into a process discussion. That is, Wanda became focused less on the pie than on her sister's tone of voice and general attitude. What she felt like saying in response was, "What do you mean, you have a *problem* with my asking you to make a pumpkin pie!? That's a ridiculous thing to say!"

If Wanda had said this, it probably would have led to a long, uncomfortable, and unproductive conversation about the conversation itself.

Fortunately, Wanda realized that nothing good would come of this, so instead, she asked a neutral question: "What kind of problem?" This was the perfect question because it allowed the conversation to go in the direction of clarifying content rather than analyzing process.

As it turned out, Jennifer had a very simple explanation. "Well, I'd just like to make something that poses more of a culinary challenge," she said. And with her answer, the conversation took off in a more productive direction.

Now, it's true that Jennifer chose an odd way of telling her sister that she'd rather bake something more challenging. She could have been much more straightforward about what she wanted. So it's not that Wanda wasn't justified in feeling upset during the conversation. But it was to her credit that she was able to avoid a fight by steering the conversation back to its original intent instead of letting it get derailed.

Be Aware of Process

Wanda and Jennifer's conversation illustrates a frequently occurring kind of situation, one in which it is far better to keep the focus on content if it is at all possible.

However, there are many times when talking about process is both helpful and necessary. Comments about process are those that supply a running commentary on where the conversation is heading; they are observations about how the speaker is feeling about the conversation, and how things are being said. It's helpful to talk about process when:

- The conversation has gotten so far off track that such a discussion is needed to get back to the content you really want or need to talk about.
- Doing so contributes to the growth of your relationship.
- It provides a way of acknowledging your sibling's efforts to be considerate.

1. Sometimes, a conversation with your sibling can become so sidetracked that you have to talk about the process of your conversation to avoid a fight. When Jack, for example, stopped talking about his business and began complaining that Stephanie was being "unethical," the conversation lost its focus on content and started to be about itself and about the process of communication. Stephanie realized that this was a shift she had to accommodate, and so she addressed Jack's concerns directly. By explaining that she wouldn't have done anything to be rude or to hurt her brother's feelings, she quickly diffused the tension and avoided more bad feelings.

2. Talking about communication process can be a way of telling your sibling something about yourself that may be so apparent to you that you have assumed he knows it, too. If, for example, you're the kind of person who asks a hundred questions, you can explain that you are motivated by a fear of misunderstanding, or because of how much you appreciate it when other people take the time to understand you. That way, your brother will understand that your persistent questions aren't simply an annoying personality quirk but that they serve a real purpose. This, in turn, will help reduce the friction between you.

3. Whenever you want to acknowledge your sibling's thoughtfulness, you're talking about process.

- I'm so pleased that you asked about my new project!
- It was so nice of you to call yesterday evening. I guess I forgot to mention that we sometimes turn the phone off during dinner and turn it back on at eight.
- I actually do appreciate your advice about my hairstyle. I have to admit that I'm a bit touchy about it since I noticed the gray streaks; I'll probably be a lot more receptive in a couple of months.

Nonverbal Communication

When you talk to someone face-to-face, your tone of voice, facial expressions, gestures, and posture say as much about you and how you are feeling as do the words you utter, perhaps even more. Although we rarely think about these nonverbal channels of communication, they powerfully affect all relationships and all communication.

Nonverbal signals communicate interest, affection, and concern as well as boredom, hostility, and bossiness. They influence the process of communication in ways that language can't. Our lack of awareness of these signals makes them more powerful, not less so. For all these reasons, it's important to learn about nonverbal channels of communication and how they affect every moment we spend with the people closest to us.

Three Truths about Nonverbal Communication

Despite all that has been written about nonverbal communication, three misconceptions abound. It has become popular to speak and write about verbal communication and nonverbal communication as if they were two different processes. However,

> 1. *No form of communication between people is either solely verbal or solely nonverbal.*
> When two or more people are talking, communication occurs on several levels and through several channels at once. Both verbal and nonverbal channels are operating all the time.

> 2. *Many people think of nonverbal communication as restricted to those aspects of communication that have nothing to do with language, but the category is actually much broader than that.*

The strictly verbal component of communication may be thought of as the part of a particular communication that can be captured on a transcript. If you talk with your brother or sister, record the conversation, and transcribe it, lots of information is missing: vocal tone and pitch, phrasing, the way that some syllables are stressed and others are unstressed, gestures, facial expressions of emotion, and how close together or far apart you were standing or sitting. Nonverbal channels of communication are not limited to visual communication—to gestures, facial expressions or "body language"—but include all those aspects of speech that would not appear in that imaginary transcript, especially the ways in which the words are said.

3. *Not everyone is equally skilled in nonverbal communication.*

The ability to discern subtle cues in the way that another person speaks is more gift than skill: some people are born with it; others are not. If you have this gift, you may erroneously assume that your feelings are as apparent to your brother or your sister as are theirs to you. On the other hand, if you do not have this particular gift, you may miss lots of information about your brother's or your sister's reaction to things you say and do as well as information about their moods.

   The answer to both problems is the same: consider your sibling's perspective. If you have the gift and your sibling does not, take the time to explain yourself clearly and be sure not to overreact if he does not intuit your every mood and feeling. If you are among the many without this particular gift, you may not always be able to intuitively understand where your brother or sister "is coming from," so be sure to ask. If you don't understand the response, ask again. If your sister grows exasperated by your questions, explain that you're asking because you really want to understand her. She'll be much more patient with your questions.

Learn Nonverbal Signals and Their Meanings

Fortunately, some nonverbal channels of information, such as facial expressions, posture, and gestures, are much more readily monitored and changed. I am including the following list of nonverbal signals and their typical meanings with some trepidation: they can easily be misused in ways that cause, rather than solve, problems. Use them to learn more about how you communicate and how you can change your behavior so that the nonverbal signals you send carry the messages you want them to. Use them to better understand your reactions to your brother and sister. Do not use them to one-up or criticize your siblings (or anyone else).

Tips for noticing and changing posture and gestures

- If your brother sits or stands with his arms crossed over his chest, he may be feeling the need to defend himself against what he thinks is your verbal assault. Find another, less threatening way of getting your point across.
- In a touchy discussion with a sibling, don't stand if he or she is seated: your sibling will feel that you are trying to dominate him or her.
- Don't be surprised if your brother or your sister reacts negatively to your finger pointing; it is a universally accepted sign of authoritarianism.
- If you notice that your sibling is making small kicking motions with her foot while you are speaking, stop and

ask her what she thinks; she is probably feeling impatient.

- If your brother shakes his head from side to side while listening, he is communicating rejection of what you said, even if he agrees verbally.
- It's best to leave the William F. Buckley Jr. posture (listening with head tilted back, eyes slightly closed) to Mr. Buckley, as many people will feel that you are only waiting for them to finish what they are saying so that you can shoot it down.

Nonverbal Channels Are Active Even When You Can't See Each Other

Telephone salespeople are often told to smile when they are talking to a hot prospect. This seems like a silly idea; after all, the person on the other end of the phone line can't see the smile. But those who teach salespeople know that we can all "hear" a smile, even when we're not face-to-face. There's nothing mystical about it: the muscles that contract when you smile affect how you sound.

Exercises:

- The next time you are talking on the phone with a friend, imagine the facial expressions your friend would express if you were facing each other. Then ask if he is smiling, frowning, or if his face is neutral. Most people are unaware of their own facial expressions. You may want to ask your friend to glance in a mirror so he or she can give you an accurate report.

   Consciously decide that you will not smile while talking with a friend. After a few minutes, ask your friend how you sound, what he or she thinks your mood is. Very often the response will be that you sound "serious," preoccupied," or perhaps "tired."

Don't Forget Touch

Touch—and I mean plain touch, not massage or acupressure—is a very powerful way of communicating. When words fail, or when more words seem to create more tension and distance, a pat on the back, an arm around the shoulder, or even a hug may be the perfect way to diffuse tension and reestablish a connection. This idea may sound like what a psychologist I know once referred to as "hot tub therapy," but it isn't.

Parents touch and hug their children, lovers express affection physically, but brothers and sisters rarely touch each other except perhaps a hug in greeting. As you'd expect, gender differences exist: sisters are a bit more inclined to touch each other; brothers are much less so, at least in the United States.

A great deal of research has shown that human touch (even as little as the touch of a cashier's hand when giving a customer change) produces beneficial psychological changes. Give it a try.

Exercise:

- The next time you are with your brother or your sister and have that uncomfortable feeling—one that arises from longing for more closeness, combined with anxiety—think about bridging the gap by touching her. If you know your sibling is sensitive about being touched, even on the shoulder or arm, ask first.

Action Steps for Improving Your Communication Skills

• Think more about what you can do to change how you communicate with your brother or your sister than about what you wish they would do differently.

• Do not make the mistake of judging what you do solely on how your sibling responds to it.

• Do not label your sibling's nonverbal behavior gratuitously ("You're assuming that authoritarian posture again!", "When you look at me that way I can tell you're not listening!").

• Learn to discuss how communication might be improved ("It's so much easier for me to listen carefully to you when we're both sitting down like this. When you stand over me, I find it harder to listen").

• Remember that the purpose of communication is not to establish your authority, affirm your superiority, or to intimidate, but is to draw the two of you together, to establish a connection. If you bear this in mind, the quality of your communication with your siblings will improve as if by itself.

• When you think that your brother or sister has insulted you, ignored you, neglected you, or unfairly criticized you, check it out before you react. Maybe he or she did, but it's also possible that the problem exists in how you are communicating, not in what he or she meant to say.

Chapter 5

Freeing Yourself from Resentment

It's all too easy for siblings to blame each other, or to blame their parents, for poor sibling relationships. But blame is corrosive. It's important to move beyond resentment and blame—and to find ways to change.

Blaming Parents

No one can deny that parents are crucially important to every aspect of young children's lives, including their relationships with their siblings. In my previous book, *Beyond Sibling Rivalry,* I strongly supported the idea that it is the responsibility of parents to do whatever they can to teach, model, and encourage their children to find healthy, loving, and mutually supportive ways of relating to each other. To the extent that parents fail to do this, and certainly to the extent that parents consciously or otherwise undermine positive sibling relationships, they are responsible for their children's conflicted relationships.

When siblings reach adulthood, however, they have achieved relative independence and are able to make their own choices. *In adulthood, our past relationships with our siblings may be due to what our parents said or failed to say, what they did or failed to do, but our present relationships with our siblings are up to us. Continuing to blame parents never helps sibling relationships improve and can even make them worse.*

When Parents Play Favorites

Some of the most lingering resentment between siblings exists because they were compared as children, with one appearing to be the "favorite." Comparisons are probably the single greatest cause of sibling rivalry in childhood—and harm everyone involved. It's clear to the less favored sibling that she got a raw deal, and she thus suffers a loss of self-confidence.

What's less obvious is that favored siblings were also harmed and suffered, too.

- They worry that although most comparisons are favorable to them, some may be negative.
- They feel guilty.
- They worry about living up to high expectations, especially when they are told things like, "Dad and I are so proud of you. We just wish your brother could be a serious student like you."
- They have trouble accepting their limitations—and those of others.
- They become easily depressed over small setbacks.

So while many siblings who were compared in these ways end up resenting each other, it's important to remember that:

- Children do not set up comparisons with their siblings; parents do. None of this was your sibling's idea or within his control.
- Holding on to blame and resentment rarely helps the situation, nor does it make you feel better.
- You may not be the only one who got the raw end of the deal. The "favored" child also carries a burden, too, sometimes one that is greater than that of the other children in the family.

Getting Over Blame

Breaking the habit of blame over being compared is difficult for several reasons. For one thing, old habits die hard. If you come from a family in which you and your sibling were always pitted against each other, then there's a good chance you are still be competing—even if it's only to be the less "bad" sibling.

Alicia and Luke's Story: "I May Not Be Perfect, But I'm Better Off Than My Sibling Is."

Alicia and her brother Luke, for example, agreed that their father was an extraordinarily difficult man and had been a disappointment as a father—absent, self-absorbed, and overly critical. As adults, they were both still frustrated in their attempts to extract any words of recognition, acknowledgment, or affection from him.

In fact, most of their communication with their father was negative. He routinely complained about one sibling to the other. But instead of uniting Alicia and Luke, it drove them further apart. Alicia put it like this: "If this is how he talks about my brother to me, imagine what he's saying about me to him!" Unfortunately, this was the only solace she could find in her relationship with her father—that he was saying worse things about her brother than he was about her.

Luke felt the same way. In the absence of cake, they fought over the crumbs. The result was protracted competition of the worst sort. It was not as obvious as it had been when they were young children and then teenagers, but, for all that, it was more insidious. Unlike the superficial competitions of their childhood years, this competition ran deep, fueled as it was by each sibling's need to have something they had never received—their father's approval.

Things didn't improve until Alicia, and then Luke, realized that they were battling for turf that neither of them controlled or ever would control. They also realized that their competition was actually keeping them from facing and at least trying to resolve the hurt and pain that both felt in connection with their relationships with their father.

Free Yourself from Resentment—Awareness Isn't Enough

It seems intuitively obvious that the more aware siblings are of what their parents did to foster competition among them, the better they will be able to overcome those competitive feelings. In real life, this doesn't seem to work out so neatly.

Bob, for example, grew up feeling as if their mother preferred his sister, Valentina. Valentina felt that their mother preferred Bob. Their mother encouraged them to compete for her affection. Both were aware of this insidious pattern and, when alone or with friends, could think about it with detachment and an almost scientific objectivity. Each could lucidly point out what their mother had done, sometimes what she continued to do, to put them at odds with each other.

But their awareness of their mother's machinations to pit them against each other didn't help them change their relationship. Even when Bob and his wife experienced marital problems because of this, he was unable to change. (Bob's wife, Ruth, a single child, couldn't stomach the fact that Bob and Valentina couldn't make up; to her, having a sibling was a gift and Bob and his sister were throwing it away.)

It seems logical that the children would find common ground in joining forces against their manipulative mother. But quite often, this doesn't happen because of the depth of loyalty children feel to their parents.

Parental Loyalty, Bonding, and Attachment

Loyalty to one's parents is an enormously powerful force in family life. I don't know if there is a physiological or a genetic component to this phenomenon, but people behave as if there is one. I've seen it in very young children, and I've seen it in adults of all ages.

Every child naturally grows up with a preferential attachment to at least one adult, and often two or more. Just as a baby duck imprints on its mother, human babies bond with their parents. The phenomenon of bonding is universal and is crucial to normal development. Children who, because of trauma, neglect, or the absence of a consistent, nurturing adult, are unable to form this first intense attachment are spoken of in the jargon of psychology as having a reactive attachment disorder. They are profoundly impaired in their capacity to form other relationships, often for the rest of their lives.

Loyalty isn't a simple concept; in fact, there are two distinct types of loyalty.

Visible loyalty

My teacher Ivan Boszormenyi-Nagy and his colleague Barbara Krasner first described the two phenomena of visible and invisible loyalty. In short, loyalty theory argues that the next generation naturally wants to be like the earlier generation in as many ways as possible. Children who are attached to their parents want to emulate their parents' attitudes, values, beliefs, and often their lifestyles as well.

If parents provide enough of what children need—love, instruction, encouragement, support, and physical presence—then attachment leads to good outcomes: children reciprocate the outpouring of parental affection and concern, and express their loyalty to their parents directly and clearly, right on the surface, for all to see. When these children grow to adulthood, they typically espouse the same values and share the same religion as well as enjoying similar recreational activities and voting for the same political candidates.

Most important, this kind of unfettered loyalty doesn't get in the way of other relationships, including relationships among brothers and sisters. People who are connected warmly and closely to their parents are able to discharge their loyalty obligations in ways that leave them free to be who they are.

Invisible loyalty

Other people are less fortunate. Their relationships with their parents are so bad that all they can think of is how to create greater distance from them. People who have had this kind of unfortunate family life, and I've met many, want to be as different as possible from their parents in as many ways as they can.

However, Boszormenyi-Nagy observed that people who reject all outward signs of loyalty are often loyal in ways that are not obvious, but are nonetheless real, and coined the term "invisible loyalty." People from families to whom they are invisibly loyal often experience chronic difficulties with close interpersonal relationships, including both sibling relationships and adult peer relationships.

This happens for two reasons. First, invisible loyalty creates a vicious cycle. People who can't acknowledge their loyalty to their parents are unable to leave home emotionally, which cripples them in their ability to form other important and positive relationships that could ultimately give them the strength to leave home emotionally.

Second, these people tend to find fault with everyone, which makes them hard to be with. But the fault finding serves an important purpose for them: if everyone is flawed, then their parents aren't so bad. In this sense, invisible loyalty is a solution to a conflict: it allows children to preserve their connection with a disliked parent and continue to dislike him at the same time. When Bob and Valentina fight and complain about each other, it's as if they are saying: "It's not just Dad who is self-centered and obnoxious; everybody is like that, especially you." In other words, if everyone is pig-headed, it's not such a big deal that Dad is pigheaded. If everyone is manipulative, it's not such a big deal that Dad is manipulative. If everyone is a nasty gossip, it's not such a big deal if Dad is a nasty gossip.

Learn to Exonerate Your Parents

The answer to this quandary—recognizing parents' responsibilities while realizing that it is futile to continue blaming them—is to gradually learn enough about your parents so that you can understand why they may have made the mistakes that they did. Forgiving a father or a mother who hurt you deeply at a time in your life when you were vulnerable can be exceedingly difficult. Many people can do this only after they get a glimmer of what life was like for that parent during the parent's childhood.

The process of exoneration provides a way for adults to understand and accept their parents' failings and missteps as those of three-dimensional human beings who experienced difficulties in life and who inevitably made mistakes. Exonerating your parents, like forgiving them, will free you from the burden of carrying all those resentments. It is a freeing process. It is also essential if one is to face fully one's disappointment that one's parents did not do a perfect job of parenting and that it is now one's own responsibility to improve relationships with siblings as best as is possible.

How to begin a process of exoneration

If you feel trapped by lingering resentments and are unable to simply "forgive," try these techniques.

- Ask your parent what life was like when he or she was a child. Find out what it was like to live through events like the Great Depression, World War II, the Vietnam War, or the assassinations of John and Robert Kennedy and the Reverend Martin Luther King, Jr.

• Look at a family photo album together and listen to what your mother or father tells you, not just with your ears but with your heart. Learn about what your grandparents were like as parents. Many people learn that their warm, indulgent, patient, and generous grandparent was demanding, rigid, punitive, and a bit scary as a parent of young children.

Blaming Siblings

Some sibling conflicts inevitably give rise to resentment. It's a perfectly natural feeling. But just because it's natural doesn't mean that it's right or that it will help you feel better about yourself. Just as blaming your parents for your difficulties with your sibling is fruitless, so is blaming your sibling for those conflicts. At best, it will have no effect. More likely, it will make a bad situation worse.

What to Do When Gifts Come with Strings Attached

Gift giving—and even more so, gift receiving—reactivates our childhood feelings and reactions. We revisit the familiar issues of who was favored, who got the biggest and best birthday present, and who was loved the most.

Settling an estate after a parent's death can be one of the most difficult sibling experiences of all. What you have to focus on during these times is what's most important to you—the object or the person.

Sam had given a handmade grandfather clock to his father as a sixtieth birthday gift. When his father died at the age of seventy-five, he left the clock to Sam's sister Rose, a sixties-style hippie who tried very hard to be nonmaterialistic and who told her father before his death that she didn't want any of his things because she didn't want to be "possessed by possessions." Rose decided to let an auction house sell it. Sam was understandably upset and angry.

Sam's lawyer suggested a brief consultation with a psychologist. Together, the three came up with a plan that rested on Sam's clear commitment to preserving his relationship with his sister, even if it meant losing the clock. Sam's first step was to understand that his father was probably motivated more out of stubbornness than mean-spiritedness. This allowed Sam to talk to his sister about the gift, making it clear that he respected their father's decision and that he valued their relationship. "I know that Dad gave the clock to you, it's yours now, and it clearly has monetary value," he told her. "It's special to me and I'd like to have it, but our relationship is much more special than any clock." Then Sam asked Rose if she would sell it to him for whatever amount she thought was fair. She agreed, he got the clock, and they kept their relationship intact.

What to do if you can't resolve it on your own

Sam's story could have ended very differently. If Rose was angry, she could have insisted on selling it to an antiques dealer for a higher price. She could have given it away. She could have changed her mind and decided to keep it. Sam, for his part, could have decided to take legal action, asserting what lawyers call "undue influence" and running up court costs equal to half the value of the clock.

If you find yourself in a dispute over an item of inherited property, you have three options: two legal and one psychological.

1. *Mediation* is a legal procedure conducted by an experienced mediator, often a lawyer, who sits with all the grown

children who feel that they have a claim on a specific piece of property and helps them explore strategies for resolving their dispute that they had not thought of or tried. For example, all the children may agree to a lottery for all the items in a book or an art collection so that each child ultimately receives an equal number of art objects, the specific objects determined by the lottery. Mediators are experts at coming up with creative solutions that everybody involved can agree on as fair, if not exactly what they had hoped for.

2. *Arbitration* is another type of legal procedure in which both parties agree that they will abide by the decision of the arbitrator or panel of arbitrators, who are typically retired judges. The procedure is much like that in a court of law, with each side presenting evidence and arguments. Arbitration is generally much shorter and therefore much less expensive than mediation.

- In *binding arbitration,* both sides agree that they will follow the arbitrator's ruling and that there will be no further legal action.
- In *nonbinding arbitration,* either side has the option of refusing the arbitrator's ruling and going to court.

3. The third option, *family counseling,* is one you should consider when you and your siblings are so angry that you can't even sit down to talk effectively with a mediator. The issues that brothers and sisters fight over the most after a parent's death, just as at all other times, often appear to be about money but aren't. Money is a way to argue over core feelings, such as loyalty, and acknowledgment. Because of this, the intensity of bad feelings between and among siblings is often completely unrelated to the amount of money in the will. In fact, the families I've worked with in which feelings are the most raw and grudges have been

held the longest are often those in which the estates were of a modest size.

When Your Sibling Says One Thing But Means Another

How should you handle a sister who always talks about becoming closer to you but never calls, writes, or visits? Is she telling the truth? Or is she evading the issue entirely?

For example, Suzanne and her sister Amy lived only twenty miles apart but rarely saw each other. When they did get together, Amy would invariably say something like, "We really need to get together more often." But when Suzanne tried to make a specific plan to see her sister, Amy was always busy.

Suzanne was confused because Amy always seemed so warm and sincere. Suzanne didn't think Amy meant any malicious intent, it just felt as if their relationship wasn't as important to Amy as it was to her.

My advice to Suzanne, and to other people in similar situations, is simple: make it very easy for your sibling to say yes. Ask what time, place, and activity would be best for him or her. If the answer is still consistently, "No thanks," you may have to accept the sad truth that your brother or your sister is truly not able to reciprocate your desire for closeness and sharing. If this happens, it's essential that you read Chapter 3 over again very carefully, and learn to "give yourself credit."

If you have interactions like those Suzanne had with her sister Amy, remember that you have reached out and offered to share yourself, something that many people are reluctant to do. If a close friend told you that he had done that, wouldn't your response be congratulatory as well as sympathetic that it didn't produce the desired results? Your response to yourself should be the same. It's natural and healthy to feel sad-

WHY CAN'T WE GET ALONG?

ness and disappointment whenever you reach out to someone and they pull away, especially if the person toward whom you reach is your brother or your sister.

When Your Sibling Criticizes You

Suzanne's experience with Amy was benign compared to Fran's with her brother Mike. Mike didn't even offer to get together and then renege; he said things like, "I'm frustrated and hurt that we're not closer. The problem is that you're not sensitive enough to my needs and, besides that, you're too rigid. That makes it hard for me to feel close to you."

In situations like these—and I hear about them often— one sibling complains that the reason she isn't closer to her sibling is because of the sibling's personality, attitude, or mannerisms. Most people who receive these multiple communications feel confused and angry at the same time. Let's carefully analyze these statements to see what your sibling is really saying. It won't erase your anger, but at least you'll know why you're reacting so intensely.

❖　❖　❖

- Your sibling says: "I want to be closer/spend more time together, but I can't/am not comfortable doing so because something about you and how you respond to me makes it impossible for me."
- Your sibling implies: "I am a warm and giving person. The reason I don't act that way with you is because of you. It's your fault."
- At a still deeper level of communication, your sibling is implying: "Pay attention to me. Make me feel important. Praise me for being sensitive. Help me feel that I am a better person than you."

❖　❖　❖

It's the combination of these meanings that gives you the headache, makes you feel that the lights have just been turned out, and makes you feel both confused and angry. The reason is that you have been blamed and criticized in a way that most people find hard to confront. After all, who would be so insensitive as to be angry with a brother or a sister who so sincerely (at least seemingly sincerely) wants a better relationship?

And don't be surprised if your sibling starts saying to others, "I tried to get closer to [your name goes here], and just opened my heart, but she couldn't or wouldn't respond. I just don't know what's wrong."

How should you handle this?

1. Begin with what your sibling really wants. If she really needs to feel important, let her—for what she has done right. You can say, "I think it's great that you want to work on our relationship," or something else like that that is usually reasonable. Since you're reading this book, it's evident that you, too, want things to be better between you, so say so directly.

2. Next, examine and analyze the blaming statements.

• *Check out the criticism and see if any of it has merit.* Are you too touchy, or not exactly the world's best listener? If anything your sibling says about you is true or partially true, then acknowledge what they said as potentially helpful.

• *Give your sibling the benefit of the doubt.* Perhaps he intends to offer helpful feedback and has never learned how to do so sensitively. I know this may not sound likely, but it does happen, especially if your sibling has the sort of problem with interpersonal sensitivity I discuss in Chapter 10.

- *Ask your sibling in what ways he is contributing to the problems and what he is doing or planning to do about his "issues."* If he has seriously thought about what he might do to improve things between you and has actually taken some steps to do so, then you have reason to feel encouraged. If he seems to shrug off responsibility, then you can conclude that his apparent desire for a better relationship is insincere.

Remain Optimistic

You can't be a psychologist and not believe in people's capacity to change. No matter how badly your sibling may have treated you in the past, there's always the chance that she has had a change of heart. If you're lucky enough to experience this, you'll do well to recognize and appreciate it as a genuine opportunity.

Julie and Jackie, for example, only rarely compared notes about their difficulties with their mother because the tenor and tone of these conversations was often subtly competitive, like much of the rest of the two sisters' relationship.

But Jackie had never felt the need to talk to her sister as strongly as she did when her mother left after a recent visit to her. Her mother had been terribly critical, complaining about the behavior of Jackie's children, her choice of husband, and her housekeeping habits. Jackie wanted Julie's shoulder to cry on, but she hesitated to call because she was unsure of how supportive Julie would be. In the end, she didn't phone.

Six weeks later, Julie called. She'd just been paid a visit by their aunt, who had been very critical of her. Relieved that Julie had sought her out, Jackie sympathized with her and told her sister about their mother's earlier visit. This one discussion didn't change their relationship, but it left both sisters more inclined to trust their instincts and call upon each other for support when they needed it. As Jackie explained to

PETER GOLDENTHAL, PH.D.

me, "I'm still pretty guarded, but at least I don't automatically assume that Julie will shoot down whatever I say."

Choose the Path of Least Resistance

If you're fortunate enough to have more than one sibling and want to improve your relationship with each of them, begin with the least problematic, not with the sibling who means the most to you—this can prove too complex at first. Instead, reach out to the brother or sister with whom you've had the least conflict, even if you have also had the least in common. This may be a much younger or much older sibling, the one who was in college by the time you were ten, or the one who was ten when you were in college. Because it will be much easier to talk to this brother or sister, you'll get the encouragement you need to tackle the more challenging sibling relationship. Your reaching out will also reverberate through your extended family, preparing the way for your next step.

Treat Your Sibling As You Would Be Treated

I've heard the following question countless times: "Everybody tells me how caring and sensitive my brother is; how come I never see it?"

The answer lies in the fact that many people don't believe that the Golden Rule applies to their families. People who would never raise their voices with a colleague or subordinate, fearing repercussions, routinely yell at their siblings. They mistakenly believe that there won't be any consequences for bad behavior.

Of course, the ramifications of poor or disinhibited behavior within a family are very real. They may not appear right away and they may not be tangible—like being fired, or facing a harassment suit—but they are no less real.

Respect each other's differences

You don't assume that all of your friends and coworkers will be just like you—root for the same team, enjoy the same foods, listen to the same music, or vote for the same candidates. If you expect your brother or your sister to be like you in all these respects, or even if you assume that he or she will always or often agree with you, you'll be disappointed, or worse.

Many people ask me, "We had the same parents and we're only two years apart, how could we be so different?" One reason you're so different is that your parents, and especially their parenting styles and philosophies, surely changed over time and with each child's birth. Another reason is that genetics plays a significant role in determining temperament and other important individual differences.

Just because you and your siblings have the same parents, unless you and your sibling are identical twins, your genetic makeup is different, not just where appearance is concerned but for many other characteristics and traits as well. Pediatric researchers have identified ten temperament traits that account for much of the difference in behavior among young children: activity level, regularity of bodily functioning, initial reaction, adaptability, intensity, mood, distractibility, sensitivity, persistence, and attention span.

My clinical experience tells me that many of these temperamental traits continue to have a great influence on people's responses and behaviors long past childhood.

- If your sister loves excitement and rushes to try every new thing, whether it's hot-air ballooning, bungee jumping, or hang gliding, then quickly loses interest and moves on to the next thing, try to think of these as characteristic of her temperament rather than as "immaturity."

- If your brother seems not to be bothered when the stereo is on full blast, when the salsa is too hot, or when other people cringe at his off-color jokes, he's demonstrating the behaviors of a person with a temperament characterized by low sensitivity.

It's far more productive to think of these as temperamental differences rather than as character flaws.

Accept ambivalence

A newspaper reporter recently asked me if one of the reasons for siblings having so many problems is because they're forced to interact. He voiced a feeling many people share. I can't tell you how many times someone has come to see me about a problem with a sibling and said, "My brother and I really have nothing in common. If we weren't brothers, he's not the sort of person I would ever meet or spend time with."

He is arguing that if he and his brother weren't related, they would have nothing to do with each other and so wouldn't have any conflicts. I see it differently. If you weren't related to your brother but still knew him, say, as a coworker, you wouldn't take his personality quirks to heart; you wouldn't expect him to appreciate everything you do; he wouldn't think it was perfectly okay to say whatever came into his head; both of you would make allowances for the other in the interest of getting along.

Try to take this perspective when dealing with your sibling. Learn to tolerate the ambivalent feelings you may have about him; these are perfectly natural.

Leave the door open

Sally's brother Bruce had always treated her very badly—accusing and blaming her, often irrationally—over the years.

She felt as if she needed to hold on to the relationship, though, because of her sons, who were close in age to her brother's children, and because she had no other brothers or sisters. But after twenty years, her patience was wearing thin. She was so upset by his brutal treatment that she asked him, "Why do you hate me?" His totally unsatisfactory answer was that it was because she had once put Tabasco sauce on his ice cream when they were children.

When Sally made an honest mistake, making a date with Bruce and his wife without realizing that she was already committed for that evening, she called Bruce to explain what had happened and to apologize for having to break their date. Bruce's wife expressed her anger in the crudest possible language.

By the time we talked, Sally had been hurt so deeply and so often that she truly felt she couldn't stand anymore. Clearly, she hoped and expected that I would endorse her decision to have nothing to do with him, to live the rest of her life as if she had no brother.

But I didn't immediately agree with her decision to cut her brother off. I didn't disagree that he, and his wife as well, had acted terribly. I offered no excuse for their behavior, for there was none. But I did suggest that she might do one more thing before giving up, as much for her own peace of mind as for any other reason: I urged her to send a short note to her brother, apologizing for the mix-up in her dinner invitation and saying that she would like to get together with him anytime he would like and that all he would have to do would be to call her.

Sally felt much more comfortable with this plan. It was not vengeful; it left the door open for her brother; it provided at least partial closure since she did not have to do anything else—it was now up to him.

Be the bigger person

Sometimes, the easiest way to overcome the resentment you feel toward a sibling is to simply decide to rise above it. Mark put this advice to work more directly than most people. After years of having a challenging relationship with his younger sister, he simply decided that there was nothing to be gained and much to be lost in continuing to squabble.

He stopped commenting on the times that she exaggerated her accomplishments, gossiped, flattered people she thought were important or denigrated those whom she felt weren't. "I just decided to try to be a bigger person," was how he put it. "She's my only sister. She's not going to change, and, anyway, the things she does are not really bad. I could choose to make a big deal of it or let it go and I decided it was better to let it go."

Action Steps for Positive Change

If your goal is to set a different and warmer tone for your relationship with a brother or a sister, bear these additional points in mind:

- *Offer criticism sensitively.* It's a challenge to offer a suggestion for a better way to do something when your history with your brother or your sister has been difficult, but it's worth trying. To increase your chances of success, first look inside and make absolutely certain that your motives are clean, that you don't secretly want to prove that you're a smarter or a better person. Then offer your criticism as you would a handshake, not a hammer blow. "I noticed that your sidewalk is really icy, you might want to get some salt on it before morning"; "Little Mike seems confused when you raise your voice."

• *Let yourself feel unnatural.* Remember that new ways of being and relating feel unnatural at first. Some of the techniques for improving relationships you've read about in this chapter will seem artificial initially. Don't let this dissuade you, though. As you grow comfortable with new ways of responding to challenging situations, and, as the relationship improves, this will change.

• *Don't overreact to your sibling's style.* Maybe your sister the social worker says, "I'm wondering how you're feeling about . . ." too often. Perhaps your other sister answers every question with a lecture or seems to enjoy the sound of her own voice. Your brother may make too many lists and spend too much time worrying about details; maybe he's one of those guys who has to polish his shoes every morning before he goes to the office. Any of these habits seem perfectly natural to the person who has them and can be terribly annoying to the people who don't. But none of them are damaging, mean-spirited, or hurtful. Your older brother's need to get home right after dinner so he can organize the buttons he bought at an auction is compulsive and perhaps a bit neurotic, but he's not hurting anybody. Neither is it worth making a big deal of.

• *Don't embarrass your brother or sister.* When your brother introduces you to his girlfriend or business associate, don't start telling "amusing" stories about his foolish escapades as a teenager or how terribly shy he used to be. If you feel an uncontrollable urge to tell stories like this, your real motive is to inflict pain, not to amuse.

• *Forget revenge.* Despite what you may have heard or read, revenge is not a dish best served cold. It is rather a dish sure to cause serious indigestion whenever it is served. My advice is to stay away from it as if it were a plate of suspicious-looking oysters in a cheap restaurant.

- *Be honest*. Mark Twain, one of my favorite psychologists, advised people to tell the truth so that they wouldn't be in the awkward position of having to remember to whom they told which story. It's tempting to cover a mistake, a forgotten promise, or an indiscretion with a lie. I suggest that anyone who thinks this is a good plan consider how successful various national leaders have been in trying to cover up their errors.

Chapter 6

How to Break
Destructive Patterns

*As they step into the same rivers, different and different waters
flow.*
—Heraclitus, as quoted by Arius Dydimus (1st century B.C.E.)

Those who study brain development tell us that every life experience produces changes in our neural connections, which in turn influence future experience. These changes in brain organization enable us to walk, talk, read, and learn.

Positive and negative life experiences also produce neural changes that continue to affect how we see, understand, and react to the world. If you and your brother have a history of squabbling, then it's altogether likely that you expect him to give you grief when you express an opinion or initiate a conversation.

And yet, it's possible to learn new ways of responding—as long as you recognize that it will require a good deal of self-awareness, considerable effort, and patience.

We often fall back on old patterns of behavior with our siblings when we:

- Resort to childhood roles
- Turn a sibling into a parent
- Gossip
- Make assumptions

- Think in terms of black and white
- Cling to expectations

Replaying Childhood Roles

As adults, we carry our pasts with us. I'm sure you've experienced the phenomenon of walking into your parents' home and feeling something change within you. Maybe you hear yourself whining, as you did when you were younger. Maybe you expect your parents to anticipate your every need. It's often exasperating to feel this way—after all, you've achieved adult relationships with everyone else in your life. But when it comes to relating to our parents, regression like this is perfectly normal.

But we also regress with our siblings. Often, this happens most when we are together, with our parents. All the old cues are present, and many times we cannot ignore them.

The Powerful Pull of Old and Familiar Cues

Twenty-five-year-old Maria and her twenty-seven-year-old sister Sheryl live in the Philadelphia area and are often the closest of friends. But when their parents come to visit, they begin to snipe at each other as if they were five and seven. These evenings together usually start well enough, but when the conversation turns to the subject of how the two sisters are doing in their careers, they both begin to feel and act jealous. They interrupt each other and frequently make snide comments.

This happens because all the old cues are there: their parents ask the same questions about their careers, and in the same ways, that they had asked about school so many years before. Naturally, these questions trigger the same jealousy and competition for parental attention as they had when the girls were young. Because neither woman felt truly self-confident, accomplished in her career, or truly happy, they were especially vulnerable to their competitive feelings.

When Maria and Sheryl were children, it was their parents' responsibility to be there to help them sort things out and to step in when needed to help them develop healthy self-esteem, self-confidence, and a sense that cooperation pays off in the long run. When their parents failed to do this—and they failed often, even failed to try often, no one would have blamed two little girls for reacting badly.

But there's a big difference between the competitiveness that arises among siblings when they are children and when they are adults. When Maria and Sheryl were children, their parents should have helped them sort things out—by stepping in when needed to help promote healthy self-esteem, self-confidence, and the sense that, in the long run, cooperation pays off. But when siblings grow up, it's up to them to learn a new way of relating.

Nothing changed for these sisters until Cheryl decided to seek therapy for herself. Her problem at the time wasn't her sister, but a boyfriend with whom she'd just broken up. Yet, in time, Cheryl gained valuable insights into herself that changed—and improved—her relationship with her sister.

How to Leave Childhood Roles Behind

Therapy can be helpful, but it's not the only way to learn to leave your childhood roles behind. Here are some other suggestions:

- *Monitor your emotional reactions, especially anger and anxiety, carefully.* Notice when you begin to become emotionally aroused. Learn to be aware of things like your throat tightening, your arms or hands tingling, more rapid heartbeats, or quicker breaths. The idea is to notice very small changes before they become runaway emotional reactions.

115

• *Remember that your family cannot read your mind.* There are two important implications of this:

1. If you are beginning to feel uncomfortable, take a moment to manage your difficult feelings before saying anything. Your family won't notice.

2. If you want your family to know how you are feeling or what you are thinking, you'll probably have to tell them.

• *Try being different and see what happens.* If you know that your family sees you as "too intense," rather than trying to convince them that they're wrong or that they should be more intense, be the laid-back one for an evening. If they think of you as "the quiet one," even though you're not especially quiet in other situations, be more talkative. If they see you as always taking everything so very seriously, make a point of laughing everything off.

• *Try pretending.* Because you are so used to acting in certain ways around your family, any change will initially feel foreign to you. If you wait to make a change until it feels natural, you'll probably have to wait a long time. Instead, pretend that you feel differently, and act accordingly. If, for instance, you want to overcome feeling personally attacked by every minor criticism, laugh them off even if you're not feeling amused. If you want to learn to feel comfortable in being more assertive with your family, be assertive first; you will soon become more comfortable with it.

When a Sibling Becomes a Parent

There are other roles that siblings take on as a result of childhood patterns. In some families, parents do their children harm by making them responsible for adult feelings and issues. It's always a misuse of power for parents to parentify children. Children never choose to be parentified and never benefit from it.

Parentification is not limited to adult-child relationships, though. Siblings can parentify each other, too, and do. Sometimes these roles are thrust on each other; at other times, a sibling can choose to let himself be parentified.

Larry and Paul: "You Do It!"

Paul and his brother Larry were part owners of a fishing cabin in Vermont. They and the other shareholders divided the responsibility for various tasks on the cabin and its associated property. Paul and Larry drew the job of finding a contractor to install a new septic system that would meet the latest, more stringent environmental codes.

When talking with Larry about progress on this project, Paul mentioned that he had spoken with a neighbor on the river about their plans to build a miniature sewage-treatment plant. Larry reacted with considerable upset: "You've gotta be careful who you talk to about this. It's a very delicate business. If word gets out that we're not up to code, we could be in real trouble. I've been working to keep this going smoothly. I wish you'd just leave it to me!"

Paul told me later that he felt his gorge rise and that he began to respond harshly: "Then go ahead and take care of it yourself!" But he was able to stop himself halfway through that statement (he remembered that what we leap to say when we're angry is probably not the best thing to say). Instead, he said something softer—"Maybe that would be best, if you could just take care of it and I'll handle something else"—and that made all the difference. He was also able to recognize Larry's anxiety enough so that he could add, "I don't think we need to worry about the neighbors; they're all going through the same thing with the new rules."

Paul let himself be parentified by his brother Larry when he responded to Larry's upset and anger with reassurance rather than reciprocal anger. Larry, in turn, allowed himself to be parentified by assuming all the responsibility for negotiating all the various regulations involved in gaining approval and installing a new septic system in an environmentally sensitive area.

To maintain a good relationship with Larry and sidestep an unnecessary conflict, Paul chose not to defend himself; instead, he acquiesced, assuming a disproportionate share of the responsibility for smoothing things out between them. Turning oneself into a parent can be a helpful strategy at times; asking your sibling to become a parent isn't.

Gossip: A Dangerous Addiction

Gossip is universal. We love to talk about other people behind their backs, and we love to listen when other people do so. If we didn't, *People* magazine would be out of business.

But some people are addicted to gossip. They don't squander their children's inheritance or break any laws; they simply talk compulsively about people behind their backs. But gossip has serious consequences. Although there is no twelve-step program for it, and no recovery movement, there should be.

What we learned as children—"Sticks and stones may break my bones but words will never hurt me"—is not true. Words can and do hurt deeply and the hurt often lasts far longer than a broken bone. When you say something negative about your brother or your sister, you have started a chain reaction over which you have no control. The most obvious damage is done when the gossip gets back to its object, with your name attached.

But this is only the most obvious bad outcome. Many times, the repercussions of gossip echo through a family without anyone realizing it. Whether the subject of the gossip is true or not doesn't really matter. This is not a legal issue of libel or not libel. It is rather an interpersonal and, in some ways, an ethical issue.

If you know you're guilty of gossiping and all of us are to a greater or lesser degree, try these techniques.

How to Break the Habit of Gossip

• Be aware of your addiction. Simply recognizing your inclination to gossip will help you be more aware of it.

• Think about the long-term and very long-term consequences of what you are about to say and weigh those against the very short-term gratification. Gossip is fun. It's fun to do and fun to hear. It also gratifies a need that most of us have from time to time to feel superior to other people. That's why it's so hard to stop. If you think carefully about the harm that might come from what you are about to say, it makes stopping much easier.

• Once you've reformed, be prepared to encounter some backlash. If you say that you don't feel comfortable gossiping, people will probably tell you it's no big deal and that you should "lighten up." Find a way to reply that feels right to you. Sometimes responding with a brief explanation or gentle humor helps.

How to Respond to Criticism

One of the most common and yet most destructive ways to respond to criticism is to become defensive. The words you use can be polite and sophisticated or basic and crude, but whenever you find yourself saying, "You do, too," or "What about the time when you . . . ," you're being defensive.

It's important to find another way to react and respond to criticism.

Although it's important to be cautious about assuming that any negative comment or so-called constructive criticism from a brother or a sister is 100 percent accurate, neither is it a good idea to assume that it's baloney. Being defensive is never helpful.

Think about it this way:

• If your brother's or your sister's critical comment is just so much gratuitous negativity, if it has nothing to do with you, there is no need to defend yourself.

• If, on the other hand, it contains even a tiny grain of truth, it's worth thinking about.

In either case, the best response is the one used by Tom, a man who came to see me recently. His brother had confronted him by saying, "You talk too much. It's as if I can't get a word in edgewise. And when you do say something, all you do is give me advice. You're not really supportive."

Tom, my client, thought about this for a moment and then responded simply and disarmingly: "You know, you might be right."

But what's really important is what he didn't say. Though he thought about adding, "And what about you?," he didn't, even though he definitely felt that his brother was project-ing—that is, his comment about talking too much had more to do with Tom's brother than with Tom.

Why didn't Tom say what was on his mind? Simply be-cause he had the wisdom to realize that no good would come of it. If, as he suspected, his brother was talking just to hear his own voice and was being critical mostly to gain attention and enhance his feeling of self-importance, then it was better to let him say what he needed to. "Besides," Tom explained to me, "maybe he is right, in which case it doesn't hurt me to give him the benefit of the doubt."

Tom's persistent commitment to avoiding defensiveness accomplished several things.

- It diminished his brother's enthusiasm for being critical just for the fun of it.

- It politely frustrated any motives that his brother might have had to upset Tom, to generate excitement, or to get Tom to bend over backward to prove that he really did care.

- It didn't reinforce what could have been construed as a mild taunt.

- It acknowledged that there might be some truth to what his brother was saying about his tendency to talk at length, allowing Tom to quietly and politely accept the possibility that he was not perfect—which is always good to acknowledge.

Making Assumptions

People get in all sorts of trouble in close relationships because they assume that things should be a certain way. It's particularly tempting to do this with your sibling—after all, who knows her better than you do?

You can diminish the extent to which your judgment is clouded by assumptions by reading through this list and honestly asking yourself how many of these statements you believe.

- I shouldn't have to apologize to my brother or my sister. This is the sibling version of "Love is never having to say you're sorry."
- My sibling should always know what upsets me and remember not to do it.

- My sibling should be more considerate.
- It's important to challenge any possible affront!
- The best defense is a good offense.
- It's essential that my brother or my sister approve of all my decisions and opinions.
- Any challenge of my beliefs or values is intolerable!
- Never trust anybody!
- I must be the richest, best looking, and most popular of my siblings!
- My siblings should always remember my birthday, my anniversary, and my children's birthdays!

Notice how many of these contain the word "should." This word, by itself, is responsible for a lot of unhappiness in relationships, especially when it is connected to the words "you" or "they." There are several ways to break the "should" habit.

Think in Terms of Preferences

Albert Ellis, Ph.D., a psychologist with an international reputation, has written extensively about how being dominated by "shoulds" can make people truly miserable. Dr. Ellis recommends that statements that contain "should" or "must" be replaced by preferential statements.

For example, suppose you're horribly upset with your brother, on the verge of getting into a physical fight with him.

- What you want to say to yourself is: "My brother shouldn't talk to me that way! I won't put up with it! I'll show him!"

- What you can say instead is: "I really wish that my brother wouldn't talk to me like that. I'll have to think of some way to talk to him about it."

Or suppose that you wish your sister would support you more.

- What you want to say to her is: "You should agree with me when I tell you about an argument I had with my boyfriend."

- What you can say instead is: "I wish you'd agree with me," or, "I'm disappointed that you don't see it my way."

Reconsider the Offense

Before allowing yourself to get upset, ask yourself if what your sister just said or forgot to say, what your brother did or refused to do was really the most horrible, awful, unbearable, "I-couldn't-live-with-it" thing to ever happen to you. Consider the possibility that it was merely disappointing, unpleasant, uncomfortable, troublesome, and not the sort of thing you would have chosen to have him or her do or say.

Consider Alternate Possibilities

Remember that there is a big difference between your brother or sister sometimes (or even often) doing or saying things that you intensely dislike and his or her being a BAD BROTHER or a BAD SISTER. Ask yourself frequently, "Is it really true that just because my brother or sister does insensitive and hurtful things from time to time that he or she is a horrible person?"

Avoid Categorical Thinking

Before I discovered psychology, I was a philosophy major in college and, as such, was taught to venerate the Greek philosophers, especially Plato and his student Aristotle. Aristotle's ideas especially have become a part of everyday thinking and have been accepted as "common sense."

But Aristotle was wrong. Things aren't either true or false; they can be both. When you think of your brother or your sister in absolute terms, you're missing a great deal of complexity. Let me explain.

Aristotle's laws are all dichotomous in nature. This means that there are only two choices: a thing is either true or it is not true. Nothing is "sort of true," "relatively likely to be true," "usually true," or "more true than not." Aristotle described three general laws:

- The *law of identity* says that a thing is always itself: a rose is a rose; a mackerel is a mackerel.

- The *law of the excluded middle* says that a thing either is something or it isn't: an animal is alive or it isn't, it is a mammal or it isn't, it is capable of having offspring or it isn't.

- The *law of noncontradiction* says that a thing can't have both a certain identity and not have it: a specific animal can't be both a dog and a cat (non-dog), a person can't be both alive and dead (non-alive).

These laws seem perfectly sensible and intuitive, which is probably why they've been around for so long. They also have a very "scientific" feel to them. In fact, writers early in the twentieth century used to say that no science would be possible without this sort of "A or not A" logical analysis.

There is a major problem with the laws, though: they do not describe all phenomena accurately. They work well for categorizing most animal and plant species. But there are species that seem to have the characteristics of both animals and plants. There are also physical phenomenon that late-twentieth-century scientists described that clearly show the limitations of Aristotle's three laws. Starting with Jan Lukasiewicz in the 1920s, philosophers have developed systems of logic that include many possibilities other than "true" and "false." Some of these logical systems contain a third term; others have multiple probabilistic statements, specifying varying degrees of truthfulness.

Physics provides other examples. At one time, physicists believed that electrons were discrete charged particles that either were or were not at certain specifiable locations on electron rings, the rings themselves being at specifiable locations. Newer models of the physical environment replaced those yes-no statements with statements about the relative probabilities of a charge being concentrated in one place or another. Physics moved from a yes- (the electron is there), no- (the electron is not there) model to a more detailed and more accurate one (it looks like a charge is there a lot of the time, but not all the time).

As I've said before, people's actions are far more complex than the movement of particles or charges, and, at least so far, impossible to predict mathematically. If physicists have to use probability statements to accurately describe the objects, forces, and phenomena they study, doesn't it make sense that we should use the same kind of statements about people? People are often both happy and sad (nonhappy), for example, at their children's high school and college graduations. Similarly, your brother can be both "a royal pain," and not a royal pain, perhaps even a "nice guy."

When you describe your brother or your sister as "obnoxious," or "nasty," or "oblivious," you can easily fall into the trap of taking your own words too seriously and believing that Aristotle's laws of identity, the excluded middle, and noncontradiction apply to you and your sibling. The risk is that as soon as you identify these features as applying to your sibling, you will believe that it isn't possible for him to be obnoxious sometimes and pleasant at other times, nasty in some situations and kind in other situations, selfish at some times and generous at other times, or aware at some times and oblivious at other times. Although there are people whose entire being is dominated by one or more of these negatives—you will read about some of them in Chapter 10—most people's behavior varies a lot from one situation to another and from one time to another.

To the extent that you fall into the trap of thinking of your brother or your sister as invariably acting in a certain (unpleasant) way, you'll miss opportunities for positive change, and for healing.

Distinguish Between Processes and Objects

One way to avoid falling into Aristotle's trap is to not confuse ongoing processes with objects.

A great danger in all challenging relationships is that of reification, or thinking of something as concrete and unchanging when it is actually abstract and fluid. If you start to think of your relationship with your brother or your sister as "damaged," you've reified it. If you think of your brother or your sister as a (you fill in the blank), you've reified him or her. If you think of your relationship with a brother or a sister as "a disaster," a "constant source of pain," or a "disappointment," you've started to think of it as fixed and permanent and impossible to change.

Don't make processes into things. As soon as you think of your relationship with your brother or your sister as "having failed," you have given up any possibility of change or improvement. If you think of that relationship as having been "very difficult up until now," or "challenging," or even "not yet where I'd like it to be," there is still a possibility of change.

How to Avoid Absolutist Thinking

- *Be mindful of situational differences.* "My brother is controlling in any situation where he has to spend money," may not seem like much of an improvement over "My brother is controlling," but it is—because it allows for the possibility that there are situations in which he is less controlling, or not controlling at all. Saying "I hate him when he acts the way he is now" (in this situation and at this time) allows for the possibility of not hating him at other times and in other situations. In thinking about your sibling, be sure to add time and situation.

• *Look out for "Doesn't everybody feel that way?" thinking.* When I challenged one of my clients about the appropriateness and wisdom of losing his temper with his brother, his response was, "Wouldn't you be upset if somebody said———to you?" Of course, my client didn't really want to know how I would feel, what he wanted to do was to make the point that his emotional outburst was "perfectly normal."

• *The same river is always changing.* Heraclitus has been famously misquoted as saying that it's impossible to step into the same river twice. This is usually interpreted as meaning that everything is always changing from one moment to the next. This sounds nice and has a pleasantly New Age ring to it. The problem is that it isn't true: your brother or sister doesn't change totally from one moment to the next or even from one year to the next. The quotation at the beginning of this chapter, "As they step into the same rivers, different and different waters flow," more accurately describes how people change over time. Their essential personality (the river) remains the same, while their specific ways of reacting and responding (the different waters) change. It's important to be aware of the distinction so that you can detect real change if and when it does occur and so you don't expect changes that will never occur.

Holding on to Expectations

Expectations powerfully color all of our perceptions. Cognitive psychologists have found that once we reach a decision or form an impression of an event or a person, we are much more likely to pay attention to evidence that bolsters our perception than we are to evidence that might cause us to question it.

Expectations, like first impressions, can also be misleading.

Nick and his sister Gerri came to see me just once for help. They weren't connecting. Nick loves thinking and talking about previous experiences and relationships; he enjoys rehashing the past. He finds it difficult to engage in pleasant, not necessarily deep or meaningful, conversation just for its own sake. He also needs a lot of reassurance that his siblings are interested in him and his activities.

However, when his sister Gerri calls and asks, "How is it going, how are you, how are the kids?," Nick doesn't think that she's really interested in knowing how he is and so he restricts himself to polite niceties and doesn't tell her what's really going on. Then he feels bad that they haven't connected.

She, on the other hand, responds to questions of that sort from friends or family with a long discourse on everything that is new in her life. To this, her brother often reacts negatively: "She gives me a lot more information than I really want. I'm really not that interested." She typically feels hurt and responds in turn, "Then why did you ask?"

After meeting several times with them, I advised Nick to be careful in what he asks for since he might really get it. I suggested that if Nick wants to be sure that Gerri is truly interested in how he is doing, that he simply ask her directly: "Do you really want to know?" If he were willing to take the risk, it would be even better to say something like, "You know, sometimes I worry that you ask but don't really want to hear. Are you sure you want to hear all of it?"

My advice to Gerri was to not blame herself for taking her brother at face value. If a close family member asks how you and your family are, he or she should be prepared to hear you out. The alternative would be for her not to ask.

If our therapeutic relationship had continued, I would have pointed out to Nick that asking his sister, "What's new?," and then complaining that she told him too much was a kind of setup. I would similarly have pointed out that choosing not to respond openly to her identical question and then complaining that she wasn't interested in him was a similar setup. Finally, if I'd felt that Nick and I had spent enough time together for him to be comfortable with a mild confrontation, I would have asked him if it was possible that he was looking for ways to validate his notions of his relationship with his sister (that she didn't really care) and of himself (that he was a better person).

Action Steps to Create Constructive Patterns of Behavior

• Remember that it is possible to change how you react, both internally and externally, to difficult situations that involve your siblings.

• Become aware of your internal dialogue about the problem situation. Tune in to those quiet voices that continue to tell you that your brother can't be trusted or that your sister is utterly selfish. Ask yourself: "Is this really still true?" Perhaps it was true when you were kids, but it's likely that she's changed as much as you have.

• Keep your ultimate goal—to enjoy a solid, mutually satisfying sibling relationship—in mind at all times. Review it before and during any encounter with a sibling that has the potential to activate your destructive ways of relating to each other.

PART 3

Help with Hard-to-Heal Relationships

Chapter 7

"My Sibling Is Just So Selfish!"

In the previous section, I suggested many techniques for improving your relationship with your sibling. I have great faith that these can help—in most cases.

However, there are some relationships between siblings that are so strained and difficult that they deserve special attention, as we will explore in this section.

"How could anyone be so unbelievably selfish and nasty?"

"Why would anyone want to be so hurtful without reason?"

"How could anyone be so blind?"

These are some of the most distressing and challenging questions people ask me about their relationships with their brothers and their sisters. They all concern the issue of entitlement.

Our Inclination to Be Generous

To understand how your sibling became so selfish, and his difficulty in appreciating your side of situations, think about what happens during childhood.

Even the very youngest child is naturally generous with other children—yes, even to their siblings—with their parents, and with other adults. While not universally true, it is very common for two-year-olds to spontaneously offer food and toys to other children, as well as to adults.

But this generosity is also fragile, a tiny trickle of water emerging from a rock in the woods. A leaf or a twig in its path can block its flow. One of the reasons I wrote *Beyond Sibling Rivalry* was to help parents of young and very young children keep this current flowing. For, once thwarted, this natural impulse toward generosity does not reemerge readily, either in children or in adults. In fact, when their early spontaneous attempts to be generous are blocked, children grow less and less inclined to try. If these same children are repeatedly hurt by life, if they experience the people around them, or even life itself, as unjust, the flame of generosity grows even dimmer.

Understanding Destructive Entitlement

For people who have been wounded during childhood, their own pain is always much more real than another's pain, even that of a sibling or other close family member. In fact, another family member's pain may be invisible. If, for example, your brother was terribly hurt as a child and received neither caring nor consideration as compensation or balm for his pain, then the risk of his being insensitive to your needs is great. Your brother may use his past interpersonal injuries to justify hurting you or another sibling. He may harden his heart so that he is unmoved by your needs or even by your suffering.

Mike's Story: "Only My Brother Can Help Me . . ."

Mike's kidneys were failing, a complication of diabetes. His only hope of regaining a normal life was to have a kidney transplant. His surgeons considered him an excellent candidate for this procedure but only if a donor could be identified whose tissues matched his closely enough. The best way to ensure such a match, as well as to obviate sitting on a years-long waiting list, is to obtain a new kidney from a living close relative. Mike's older sister had just been through a round of chemotherapy for breast cancer, his younger sister was pregnant, and his parents were elderly.

That left his younger brother, Rick, who was healthy and vigorous. Much to everyone's shock, Rick refused to even consider being a donor. His reason, which he freely offered, was that he enjoyed his rugby and competitive "masters'" skiing and worried that his athletic activities might be limited if he donated a kidney to his brother. He also expressed concern that being away from work after surgery would cost him a lot of money. The fact that Rick was pushing forty-five, an advanced age for a rugby player, or that he would still be able to play tennis, swim, ski recreationally, and run marathons did not budge him from his position. He would not consider the possibility that a relatively small sacrifice on his part would be balanced out by the huge improvement in his brother's quality of life. He felt perfectly comfortable knowing that his brother would have to remain on dialysis for at least a year, and possibly longer, while waiting for a kidney to become available.

This particular refusal to make a relatively small sacrifice so that a sibling can experience a very significant benefit is extraordinarily unusual—I've only seen it twice—but the underlying "I have to think of myself first" mentality is not. Neither is the seeming attempt to justify selfishness based on past or anticipated future discomfort unique.

Walls Built By Hurt

Rick is a person who feels destructively entitled. What do I mean by that? How could anyone possibly be entitled to be destructive? The term seems oxymoronic. The best way to explain concepts like this one is through two clinical examples.

• Many years ago I saw a nine-year-old boy with sickle cell anemia, a chronic, life-threatening illness that causes painful and frightening crises requiring hospitalization and transfusions. This child was a handful. He acted without thinking and often communicated his anger and frustration in highly inappropriate ways. During the week before I first saw him, he'd been suspended from fourth grade for threatening his teachers and his principal. When confronted, he said he would rather be dead and tried to climb out a third-floor window.

As I began to interview him, this little boy said, "I don't like this planet. It isn't fair." A shocking statement, but one with considerable truth: life had not been fair to him. He was entitled not to care about how his behavior might bother or inconvenience other people. In simple words, this little boy captured the essence of what it means to be destructively entitled.

• Arthur was a thirty-year-old man who as an adolescent had lost his sight in an accident. Prior to his accident, Arthur was a gifted painter who had a real shot at being successful in the competitive art world. When I met him, he was bitter, nasty, and critical of everyone around him: his wife, his children, and most of all a sister who had achieved what he could not.

She was a well-known designer of tapestries and custom wall coverings. Arthur was never able to offer his sister any words of acknowledgment or congratulation for her achievements. He was quick to criticize her whenever he could. When no publisher would accept her idea for a book about her designs, he brought it up every time he saw her. All this despite the fact that she was a devoted sister who had helped him and his family in many ways. That one event had shaped his life and cast a pall over it ever since. His whole life was built around his reliance on destructive entitlement.

People like this literally cannot see anyone else's point of view, cannot empathize with anyone else's difficulties or needs, and are incapable of caring about anyone else's feelings or wishes. People who rely on destructive entitlement have often been hurt by others earlier in life and use this past hurt to justify being insensitive and selfish. They say to themselves:

- I've been hurt so badly that I shouldn't have to worry about whether something I do or say might hurt anybody else.
- I have to think of myself first or nobody else will.
- How can I avoid doing the favor my sister asked of me?
- What's in it for me?

Causes of Destructive Entitlement

What causes someone to become destructively entitled? There are two reasons, and both begin in childhood.

Children who are hurt

Much of what we do as children has the direct or indirect purpose of pleasing parents. Sometimes it's very obvious: a six-year-old tries to tickle her father, who seems mopey. Sometimes it isn't at all obvious: an eight-year-old strives to make the basketball team so that Mom and Dad will be as proud of him as they seem to be of his older brother.

Children behave this way because they want attention and, even more profoundly, they want approval—they want to make their parents happy. Anyone who has spent time with children knows that they are exquisitely attuned to our moods and behaviors and will do almost anything to try to pick up our spirits if they feel this is needed. (Sometimes these perceptions are not totally accurate, but they are always powerful and children tend to act on them quickly.)

When a child pleases a parent, two things happen: the child experiences an instant boost in self-worth, and she is inclined to do something similar again. That something similar may involve being generous with a sibling.

On the other hand, a child's efforts to please her parents may have met with indifference or even punishment. If this happens repeatedly, she may grow less and less motivated to do anything nice for anyone, least of all a family member.

Some people are able to overcome even very hurtful experiences in early life and go on to be considerate and sensitive people. Many others, however, bracket off their hostilities, keeping them from intruding at work while giving them full vent with family, especially siblings. Whether they go one way or the other is influenced by temperament (more about this later), by education, and by experience.

But the unfortunate truth is that some people become so embittered that they are only able to do right when they perceive clear and imminent personal gain resulting from it.

Children who are turned into parents

Some people become destructively entitled because they were "parentified." (If you find that you sometimes have negative thoughts and feelings that run counter to your beliefs and values, feelings that you are distressed to recognize in yourself, you may be dealing with the effects of destructive parentification yourself.)

This term needs clarification. A thirteen- or fourteen-year-old who occasionally watches a younger sibling is not necessarily parentified. A child of any age who is used to meeting a parent's or other adult's emotional needs is parentified. Parentification involves a role reversal: instead of the parent concerning himself or herself with the child's emotional needs, the child has assumed the burden of worry about the parent's emotional needs.

Sometimes the burden is overt: a ten-year-old covers up his mother's alcoholism so that she will not lose custody of him and his sister. Or it can be subtler: a twelve-year-old girl has to entertain her parents and make them laugh because they seem sad much of the time. Sometimes it is both: a seventeen-year-old allows her depression to reach life-threatening levels before she asks her parents for help out of concern that they might be distressed or embarrassed by her "weakness." If you have been called upon to act like a selflessly giving parent, you have been parentified.

People who were parentified often conclude, like Arthur or the little boy with sickle cell anemia, that the whole planet was unfair to him. They feel as if they've been pushed around too much, as if too much has been asked of them.

Is Your Sibling Destructively Entitled?

Everybody occasionally does things that hurt others; this does not necessarily represent destructive entitlement, only human frailty. People who rely predominantly on destructive entitlement in relating to others, however, have experienced so much pain and injustice that they have become blind to the impact of their actions on others and blind to the harm that they cause others. Such people also seem immune to the feelings of guilt or remorse that most of us experience if we learn that something we've done has caused another person harm.

To determine whether your sibling is destructively entitled, ask yourself these questions:

- Does she show remarkably little sensitivity to or concern for your needs, feelings, hopes, or misfortunes?

- Does he act as if he were literally blind to your feelings, your hopes for the future, your regrets about the past, and those issues about which you are especially sensitive?
- Does she seem oblivious to the way that her words affect you or other people?
- Is he unaware of a tendency to ignore, belittle, or put down?
- Is she capable of hurting you (or other people) without being troubled by it?

These are the signs of a person whose approach to life is built upon a reliance on destructive entitlement. It is extraordinarily difficult to change a brother's or a sister's tendency to rely on destructive entitlement. It is still, however, worth figuring out if this pattern underlies the way they relate to you.

Managing Your Sibling's Destructive Entitlement

People rely on destructive entitlement when they feel it is the only or best way to justify what they want to do. Give them another way and their behavior might change. Whatever you do, don't try to take their entitlement away from them; they will inevitably just hold on to it more tightly. To the extent that they continue to rely on destructive entitlement, they have very little ability or freedom to give. The hurt of the past has led them to give up that freedom. Instead of asking themselves, "How can I enhance my own worth by being helpful to, or at least considerate of, my brother or my sister?," they worry, "I have to think of myself first because nobody else will."

Ashley, for example, tried to convince her sister Jerrilyn that her memories of their childhood were distorted, that any taunting or teasing had been pretty evenly divided between them. Although Ashley may well have been right by objective standards, Jerrilyn responded as if her sister was trying to take something of great value from her. She dug in her heels and recounted every occasion on which her sister had been "mean" to her, during their childhood, as if to prove that she had truly been treated unfairly and harmed. The more Ashley tried to reassure Jerrilyn that things had not been so bad, and the more she defended herself by suggesting that Jerrilyn took small things too seriously, the worse it got.

So how can you help your sibling loosen her grasp on destructive entitlement? By offering a direct, unvarnished, empathic, and supportive response, such as:

- It must have been really awful for you.
- You must have been terribly hurt for the memory to be so fresh and vivid today.
- I wish I could have done something to help you.
- I hear you saying that you're still very angry about (those events/my earlier behavior, etc.).

Say only things that you believe to be true and are able to say with sincerity. If you don't wish that you could have done something to help your sister, don't say so. On the other hand, don't hold back. If you find yourself feeling badly for your brother, say so.

It may be hard for you to say these things to your sibling. Perhaps you dearly believe that people should "get over the past and on with the future." Perhaps you believe that you are the one who deserves the apology, not your sister. Perhaps you are tired of being the one to apologize, or being the "reasonable" one. As one patient said to me, "When my brother tells me for the hundredth time that I'm self-centered and don't show enough interest in him, I don't exactly feel like telling him that I feel his pain. I feel like telling him that he *is* a pain."

I told him that there was nothing wrong with telling his brother that he was a pain but that he might get farther by first acknowledging his brother's need to be important.

If you resist saying the things I suggest, then remember this: *offering empathic support does not automatically convey your belief that your brother or your sister is right in blaming you for the past.* By empathizing, you are neither apologizing nor assuming guilt; rather, you are expressing your empathic understanding of your sister's past and present pain. You are not assuming responsibility for her pain, or even telling her that her pain is "justified." You are telling her only that you see, hear, and understand that she was and is in pain. Just that and no more.

A simple empathetic statement can have a huge effect. What I have found over the years is that if you are able to respond to your sibling in this way, things will improve between you. This happens because your sibling doesn't feel forced to give up his old pattern of behavior, his destructive entitlement, on which he has relied for so many years.

Remember, people who rely on destructive entitlement have used their history of having been treated unfairly to justify their approach to life, to relationships, and to seeking and gaining what they want, whether material or emotional. They have, in all likelihood, based their senses of themselves, their identities, on having been hurt, misunderstood, or neglected. Their "I can't think about you, I have to think about myself" mentality depends on this sort of internal justification. Acknowledging their pain is a place to start.

If you've been too badly hurt to care about your sibling or to acknowledge his having been hurt, this technique, and techniques like it, will not be for you. If, on the other hand, you're willing to try a new way of responding that has a possibility of changing things for the better and very little chance of making things worse, this technique may be for you.

The more that your brother or sister can see the future as having possibilities not presented by the past, the greater are the chances that he or she will rely on constructive entitlement. Letting your sibling know that you can see his hurt and are sympathetic will almost always lead to improved relationships.

Destructive Entitlement Isn't Inevitable

When I speak about destructive entitlement, there is always at least one thoughtful audience member who asks, "Do you mean to say that anyone who has been hurt psychologically is doomed to become selfish, self-centered, insensitive, and uncaring?"

The answer is: "Not necessarily." We have all encountered people who have experienced great personal loss, personal injustice, and even personal tragedy in their lives and who are nonetheless able to be sensitive to others and to consider how their actions will affect other people. Examples of this sort of transcendence of personal tragedy are evident in all spheres of life. The woman who founded MADD, for instance, suffered the loss of her own child to a drunk driver. Though she had every right to become preoccupied and selfish because of her grief, she, and many like her, was able to respond to personal tragedy in positive ways. Some of these people say that they are motivated by the hope that others won't have to suffer as they did.

Most likely, people who seem invulnerable to the numbing and compassion-blocking effects of personal loss have almost certainly had significant relational inoculations early in their lives. They may have had an especially nurturing and loving extended family who fostered their capacities to care about other people. Or there may have been one family member, a parent or perhaps a grandparent, whose guidance, protection, and care was sufficient to counterbalance difficulties and deprivations in childhood and later. For some people, the invulnerability did not come from a biological family member, but from a close family friend, an honorary uncle or aunt.

People whose lives are characterized by a reliance on destructive entitlement seem to be blocked in their capacity to give. People who live their lives by the principle of constructive entitlement have avoided these blockages. They have preserved their freedom to be generous, despite having suffered.

Understanding Constructive Entitlement

Those who rely on destructive entitlement take as their theme song, "It's All about Me," the refrain of which is, "I have to think of myself!"

Those who choose to rely on constructive entitlement sing a very different lyric: "What can I do that is helpful, or at least not hurtful—something that I can reflect on with pride ten years from now?" Each of these people has decided to actively look for ways to feel good about himself or herself, not by being self-indulgent, but rather by being considerate of other people, by being compassionate, by being generous, by having and showing empathy for other people, especially for other people's suffering. There is a word in Yiddish, a language rich in nuance and subtlety, that defies exact translation into English but captures this sort of person well. He or she is a *mensch,* a good person in every sense of the word.

What motivates people who are constructively entitled— people like Allison, who devoted herself completely to helping her sister through the last trimester of an especially difficult pregnancy? Or Stacie, who took time off from her psychiatry residency to be with her younger sister while she was recovering from surgery? Or Margaret, who took a leave from her job to help care for her two nieces when their mother (her sister-in-law) was diagnosed with a particularly aggressive form of breast cancer?

One great source of motivation is the opportunity to do something worthwhile, something that will contribute to improving the life of another person, of an institution, or perhaps the ecological health of our planet.

Such altruism has its own rewards. You will probably be recognized by those around you as a giving and generous person. You may, and should, feel pride in what you have done to help other people. You may also find that other people treat you well as the result of what you have done and the reputation you have gained from doing it. Thinking about the short- and long-term benefits to other people of what you do is, unfortunately, not well supported by our current popular culture of institutionalized and glamorized selfishness. That makes it even more important that you learn to give yourself credit for your considerate acts in the ways that you read about in Chapter 3.

Be Wary of Overgiving

Being generous and considerate, however, doesn't mean that you should allow yourself to be exploited. Be sure that when you do something to help your brother or your sister or to accommodate their wishes, that you do so freely, not because you feel that you must or are worrying about their anger if you don't. I've known many sibling relationships in which one person was the "giver" and the other the "taker." Whether it involved small loans that were never repaid, promises that weren't kept, or plans that were broken, the results were the same. The "overgiving" sibling eventually became resentful; the "overtaking" sibling felt more and more empty, unable to establish her self-worth.

Choosing Constructive Entitlement

You can learn to rely on constructive entitlement despite having been hurt and treated unfairly. *Whether you accrue destructive entitlement is largely out of your control, but whether you choose to base your life on that accrual is under your control.* It's not easy, but you can choose to treat your siblings better than they treat you, better perhaps than life has treated you. Although it's important to know what you are feeling, it's not always a good idea to act on those feelings.

When I began helping Rachel sort out her very complex relationship with her three younger siblings, she initially benefited from becoming aware of how burdened she felt from having been parentified all her life. It was important for her to reflect on the pervasive fatigue she felt from years of worrying about her siblings. It was important for her to realize that underlying this fatigue was considerable anger about the unfairness of her position and the expectations that had been imposed upon her.

But I did not advise Rachel to show her anger to her family, believing that this would make matters worse. Instead, I helped Rachel extricate herself from her parentified role. For most people, important and intimate relationships improve dramatically when spontaneous and natural feelings are filtered through a mesh of values and judgment.

It comes down to this: you can choose to base your choices, including your requests and demands, your generosity and selfishness, on your accumulated entitlements in one of two ways: destructively or constructively. When you do your best to consider how your statements and actions affect those closest to you, when you look for opportunities to be helpful to your brothers and your sisters (and to your spouse and your children as well) because you feel good about yourself, when you are able to contribute to others, you are relying on constructive entitlement.

When Gabrielle, for example, invited her curmudgeonly brother and his wife to join her family for Passover, she anticipated that he would turn down the invitation, or that he would participate in the seder only grudgingly. She invited him, not because she expected a positive response, but because she wanted to embrace the possibility that he would respond well.

Her brother did accept the invitation. Not only that, but he and his wife participated actively in the seder. That they did so was an unexpected bonus. What was most important to Gabrielle was that she had extended the invitation, not what happened afterward.

Exercise:

- To enhance your capacity for constructive entitlement, ask yourself the following questions:

  - How would I want my brother or my sister to respond to me if this situation were reversed?
  - What can I do to help or support my sibling that will make me feel good about myself?
  - What decision can I make today that I will feel good about in ten or twenty years?

In this way, you will increase your freedom to act in considerate and caring ways that your siblings cannot help but respond to positively. Despite themselves, they, too, may begin to consider how what they say and do affects you.

Action Steps: Learn to Rely on Constructive Entitlement

- When you make a decision to act based on your reservoir of constructive entitlement, the act is its own reward. You will immediately have more constructive entitlement.

• If you're not sure whether it's worth the effort to set aside your resentments, don't ask yourself why you should bother to do the considerate thing. Ask yourself instead what possible benefit there would be to you to do the inconsiderate thing.

• What goes around does come around. You will earn the respect and admiration of other family members and friends each time that you act in a generous (constructively entitled) way toward your siblings.

• One major benefit of actions that reflect constructive entitlement is that you'll never have to worry about what other people will think of you if they find out. Neither will you have to try to remember which cover-up story you told to which relative. This is the family version of "Never do anything you wouldn't want to read about in the newspaper."

Chapter 8

"But I'm Still Angry!"

Fear is the path to the dark side. Fear leads to anger; anger leads to hate; hate leads to suffering.

—*Yoda*, Stars Wars, Episode One: The Phantom Menace

Anger can be as addictive as alcohol. Like alcohol, it enables people to behave in ways that they wouldn't if they weren't "high" on it. Like alcohol, anger can be a shy person's best friend, breaking down barriers that otherwise exist. Like alcohol, anger can be a timid person's entry into the world of aggressiveness.

The problem lies in the fact that being aggressive isn't really the same as being assertive, and the side effects are often uncomfortable. One potential risk for the normally timid person is that of being so pushy that he or she then feels self-conscious and guilty and does too much to "make it up" to the other person, failing again to achieve a balanced relationship.

Anger is also the emotional correlate of destructive entitlement, which you read about in the last chapter. What do I mean by this?

When you rely on destructive entitlement to justify doing something you might not otherwise feel right about doing (such as not returning a brother's phone calls), you do so by thinking about all the unfair things you've experienced, all the ways that you've been hurt. Then you can tell yourself, "After all the ways I've been hurt, I don't have to observe such trivial social rules as returning phone calls or being polite or apologizing for my mistakes." That's the cognitive side of destructive entitlement.

Anger in all its varieties—rage, smoldering anger, resentment, irritation, bitterness—is its emotional side.

Anger's Destructive Wake

Hal, a second-generation businessman, called me a few years ago for a consultation. All five of his siblings were working with him in the small manufacturing company that his father had begun on a shoestring and which was now enormously successful. Yet Hal's father hadn't given much thought to what he could do to ensure harmonious relations among his children, or how his actions would affect their relationships with each other. For example, he had established a pattern of subordinate and supervisory relationships between them that was sure to cause conflict—and did. Other business decisions were based on his personal feelings, many of which reflected his baggage from a difficult relationship with his own brother.

Hal was so angry with his father and two of his siblings that it was damaging not only his business but his physical health and his marriage as well. When he came to see me, it was clear that he hoped I would be able to tell him what to do to get his father and his siblings to change, and quickly. Of course I had to tell him that I probably couldn't do that. To Hal's credit, he asked what else I might have to offer. I told him things he already knew but had not truly accepted: that he could not change anybody else, that to a very large extent how he felt about the family business and his place in it was up to him, and that he had to decide whether his health, his marriage, and his relationships were more or less important than having the role he felt he deserved in the company.

Hal was a thoughtful and reasonable person. He made what I considered the right decision, that personal and family health is more important than "winning." He decided to stay in the family business but to do so in a more detached way, so that he did not take everything that happened so personally. He decided to look at his employment as a "job," not as defining his personal worth.

After a year or so of looking at his job in this way, a headhunter approached him about a job at another large company, with a great salary, benefits, stock options, and all the rest, and he made a change. Later, Hal told me that when he was locked into his anger he wouldn't have been able to accept even such a good opportunity because it would have meant "losing." After freeing himself from the need to prove that he was right and everyone else was wrong, he was able to recognize and accept a good opportunity when it was offered to him.

How to Release Yourself from Anger's Grasp

For many people, the biggest block to moving from destructive to constructive entitlement is their own anger. Here's why: when you are angry and you hold on to that anger, you can justify doing things that you might not otherwise feel entitled to do. Some of these may be nasty or even vindictive. Others may be perfectly legitimate things that you actually ought to be doing but for some reason can't allow yourself to do.

One option open to Hal, for example, would have been to use his anger at being treated badly in the family business to justify quitting and finding other work. Quitting, by itself, wouldn't have been such a bad idea, but quitting in anger would have been destructive. Leaving because he had a better offer left him free of all the emotional and family upset that would have occurred if he had relied on resentment and anger rather than a simple economic analysis of the options.

Be assertive, not aggressive

A far better solution is to learn to be assertive. Many people think that they're capable of being assertive, but they aren't. They're just complaining. For example:

- Telling your brother, "I don't appreciate it when you cancel plans at the last minute," is a complaint.

- Telling him, "I know that sometimes in the past you've regarded plans we make as tentative. I would really appreciate your letting me know if you're thinking of this as tentative or if you can commit to it, because if you can't, I'd prefer to put it off until a time when you can," is being assertive.

Some people can be very assertive on the job but not in personal relationships. Many others are great complainers but poor askers. Fortunately, everyone can learn to be more assertive.

What is assertiveness?
Assertiveness means:

- standing up for your rights without trampling on your sister's rights.
- asking for what you want clearly and unequivocally
- being direct, and not resorting to hints or suggestions
- holding your ground even if your position is unpopular
- being in control of your emotions so you don't get side-tracked

How can you be assertive when someone continually interrupts you?

Don't say, "Will you let me finish my statement!?" This sounds assertive but it isn't. You're giving up too much power by asking, "Will you let me?" and are also becoming too emotional.

It's more effective to just keep talking as calmly as you can.

How can you be assertive when it appears as if the other person hasn't heard you?

Don't say, "I feel like I'm talking to a wall! What does it take to get you to answer me?" You're getting angry and risking losing control.

It's more effective to just repeat what you said before in the same neutral tone of voice. Be prepared to keep repeating it until you receive a direct response.

Let the Future Guide Your Decisions Today

Another good strategy to diffuse anger is to ask yourself these questions:

• What can I do today that I will look back on with pride and satisfaction ten or twenty years from now?

• What should I avoid doing today because I know that I will regret it later?

One way to make these somewhat abstract questions more concrete is to imagine scenes from your future: your fortieth, fiftieth, sixtieth, or seventieth birthday; your child's, niece's, or nephew's bat or bar mitzvah, first communion, high school or college graduation; the birth of grandchildren. To get the maximum benefit from this exercise, don't just fly through it. Instead, really think about what sort of connection you want to be able to make with your siblings at those future life events. Ponder your legacy.

Get Other People Involved

In some situations, you may be so angry with your sibling that you really can't sort out the situation without enlisting the help of others. This is particularly true in cases in which siblings have stopped talking to each other; these are referred to as "cut offs."

Michelle, for instance, told me that she hadn't spoken to her brother or been involved in his life for years, ever since she had what seemed to her to be a minor disagreement with her sister-in-law years before. By now, Michelle's feelings were so intense that she didn't know how to begin to heal the breach.

I suggested that she talk to other people in her family, someone who was close to her brother, and let them know how angry and hurt she was, and how much she wished for a reconciliation with her brother and his family. The goal is to let the intermediaries know that you don't know what you did wrong and that you're sorry if you caused hurt to your sibling or her family.

It's important that you do this assertively—that is, in a way that emphasizes your desire for healing. Don't cast blame; don't speculate about your sibling's motives. Don't blame yourself or cast yourself as a martyr or a scapegoat. In fact, don't say anything about your sibling at all: just concentrate on your feelings.

For example, Michelle could approach a favorite aunt and say, "I feel terribly hurt by all this and I'd do anything to get back together with him. If it's all about that argument ten years ago, I'm really sorry. I don't know what else to do."

This wasn't easy advice for Michelle to digest. She hated involving other people, partly out of embarrassment and partly because she didn't think anyone would want to help. But I advised her to forget about the embarrassment and to take the chance that while some people may not want to help, others will.

Stress and Anxiety Reduction

Staying angry with a sibling can be bad for your health. Recent scientific literature is full of examples. Heart attacks occur when people are angry, for example, because intense anger is a complex psychological and physiological process involving a cascade of thoughts, feelings, hormones, and neurotransmitters. The chemicals that are released when you are angry cause profound changes in your heart rate; blood pressure; the blood flow to your internal organs, skin, and muscles. Sustained anger over long periods of time significantly lowers the body's resistance to infection and disease, including cardiovascular disease.

Other research reveals that expressing all of your anger all the time isn't healthy, either.

Most people believe that they know how to relax when in fact they carry a great deal of tension around with them every day of their lives.

That's why it's crucial for everyone to learn the rudiments of relaxation.

Learning to relax

Over the years, I've combined a number of well-researched relaxation techniques into one easily learned procedure. You can follow it by yourself or, better yet, do it with someone you know and trust. You will be learning a new set of skills that will become easier with practice. As you practice the exercises, your ability to relax will increase, you will be able to achieve a greater depth of relaxation, and you will be able to do it more quickly. After practicing for several weeks, you'll notice that you'll feel the relaxation response begin sooner.

Make sure that you are truly comfortable. Your feet should be flat on the floor. If not, move to a lower seat or use a footrest. Make sure that your back is well supported. Put a small pillow behind your back if you like. The same is true for your head and neck. Many people prefer to do their relaxation breathing while sitting in a high-backed chair or on a sofa with a high back. Use a neck pillow if you like. (Once you fully master the technique, these special arrangements will not be needed, but they will make your learning process quicker and easier.)

Breathe for relaxation. That means breathing in a way that gives your body time to fully recharge itself and to reestablish normal physiological processes when they have been disturbed.

First, decide if you want to close your eyes or keep them open. If open, select something pleasant at which to direct your gaze, perhaps a painting or a photograph on a nearby wall, or even a bit of wallpaper pattern.

Take a nice, comfortable, deep breath, gently filling your lungs. Don't gasp or inhale sharply, as when your doctor requests a deep breath while listening to your chest. Rather, take in a breath deeply and slowly, breathing from your diaphragm.

Most of the time most people fill only the top half of their lungs when breathing, using the small muscles between their ribs to expand their chest and to inhale. This is really only half a breath. To get a full breath, the kind you need if you are going to learn to relax, you will need to use your diaphragm, a much bigger muscle that separates your chest (containing your heart and lungs) from your abdominal cavity. Pulling the diaphragm down is the only way to allow your lungs to fully expand and the only way to have a complete inhalation-exhalation cycle. The old saw about taking a few deep breaths when angry or upset intends this kind of breathing. Ten shallow, quick gasps will only lead to hyperventilation and increased physiological arousal, not relaxation.

The trick is to keep in mind that you aren't trying for maximum lung expansion, just for nice, easy, and full breaths. Don't hold your breath. At first it may help if you place your hand flat over your abdomen as a physical reminder to breathe using your diaphragm. When you're breathing properly, your abdomen will expand just a bit as you inhale, exactly the opposite of "sucking in" your belly. This muscle group is the only one that can accomplish the task of even, relaxed, full breaths. Let yourself rest a second or so between breaths; you will definitely not run out of air.

Now, take a nice, deep breath, pause for a second or two, then let it out. You don't have to push your breath out, just let it drift out by itself. Imagine a bicycle wheel going around and around. Your breathing should be like that, a continuous, gentle cycle. Take and release ten breaths in this way. How long did that take? Use a clock or a watch with a second hand. If your ten breaths took about a minute and a half, you're doing great. If, on the other hand, you managed to squeeze ten breaths into one minute, try to slow them down a bit. Six to eight breaths a minute is about right for most people.

Relax your posture. As you continue your breathing, let yourself sag into your chair. Feel your muscles loosening up. Feel the floor supporting your feet and the sofa or chair supporting your legs and back. You will gradually notice the easing of tension in your hands, arms, back, and neck. Feel the muscles of your face, especially those around your eyes and mouth, sagging a bit. Keep breathing, slowly and deeply.

Add visual imagery to enhance your relaxation. Still relaxing and breathing diaphragmatically, imagine yourself in a movie theater. It is absolutely new, sparkling clean, and very quiet. The seats are the most elegant, luxurious, and comfortable seats imaginable. They, too, are brand new. Your seat reclines to the perfect angle. It's very comfortably upholstered, perhaps in soft leather or plush velvet or some other especially comfortable fabric. It's a high-backed seat with full support for your neck and shoulders and head. As you sit in the theater, very relaxed, the lights dim. On the screen in front of you appear large numbers, one at a time. They may be black letters on a white background or they may be in different colors. As each number appears before you, breathe one of your deep, relaxing breaths and become more and more relaxed.

If someone is reading this to you, ask them to slowly count the numbers aloud, like this, "Number three, another nice, deep breath and feel more and more relaxed." Have them count this way, very slowly, from one to ten. By the time you get to number ten, you will be very relaxed indeed, perhaps more relaxed than you have ever been. Take a moment to enjoy the feeling, and, when you are ready, move on to the next visual image.

Imagine a place you've been or would like to visit, a relaxing, peaceful place. You might be alone, or perhaps with a few close friends. You might see water, perhaps a lake or an ocean. It might be a favorite place or an imaginary one, like the Jersey shore or the French Riviera. Picture yourself lying on that beach, on the warm, soft sand. The air is delightfully warm, a very light breeze may be blowing. Perhaps a small bird flies by. You sink into the sand, feeling more and more relaxed. Enjoy the relaxation.

As an alternative, ask a friend with a soothing voice to record the material from the preceding pages for you to listen to as you do your breathing exercises.

How your body changes during relaxation

You may not be aware of it, but during this exercise your body changed in several ways. In addition to the deepening and slowing of your breaths, your pulse and blood pressure decreased and your skin temperature increased slightly. The concentration of cortisol (the fight or flight hormone) has decreased markedly.

Here is a simple technique you can use if you're having difficulty telling whether you're relaxed or not. Buy an inexpensive indoor-outdoor thermometer. Be sure that the wire for the outdoor temperature sensor ends in a metal tip. Set the selector switch to "outdoor." Hold the probe on the end of the wire gently between your thumb and the tip of your index finger or, if you wish, tape it to the tip of your index finger with a small piece of adhesive or transparent tape. As you relax, the temperature reading will gradually increase, indicating an increase in the skin temperature in your hand. Relaxation causes dilation of the tiny blood vessels in your fingertips, allowing more blood to flow into them. This in turn increases the temperature in your fingertips.

By monitoring the temperature increase, you can get instant feedback on how well your relaxation exercises are going. An even simpler and less expensive gadget is a mood ring or mood strip, one of those celluloid strips that changes colors and has a key that equates color changes with levels of relaxation.

After practicing these techniques, you will be able to move into the relaxed-breathing modality more quickly. It's like learning a golf swing or a tennis serve: after a while, it becomes automatic. And just as with these athletic skills, relaxation skills are best practiced away from the course and the courts and during nonstressful moments. Then you can call on these learned skills when you need them. Although it may take you ten to twenty minutes to get into a state of deep relaxation the first several times you try the exercises, before long this time will decrease and with practice you will be able to enjoy deep relaxation within one or two moments of beginning your breathing routine.

Thought control

These breathing and imagery techniques are sufficient for many people. Others, however, need something extra to help them relax. Among the techniques that my patients have found most helpful is one borrowed from rational-emotive therapy, a treatment approach developed by Dr. Albert Ellis.

This technique gives you a way to more carefully examine your own reactions to events so that you can begin to gain control of those reactions.

In short, I advise you to ask yourself these two questions when you find yourself upset about something your sibling has said or done:

- Is this a calamity, a catastrophe, and a "terrible" thing or is it unpleasant, aggravating, disappointing, and not at all what you would have preferred to happen?
- What's the worst thing that might happen?

Here's how the technique works. Robin's brother suddenly threatened to sue her for repayment of a fifteen-thousand-dollar loan he'd made to her years before with the understanding that payment could wait as long as she needed it to. Robin was overwhelmed with hurt, anxiety that she might not be able to pay the loan back, and fury with her brother, whose income was easily ten times hers.

I asked Robin, "Is this truly the end of the world, the worst possible thing that could happen to you or your family?" When she said it wasn't, as I knew she would, I then asked, "Is it more like a truly unpleasant, aggravating, annoying thing that you really wish hadn't happened and that you would greatly prefer not to happen again if possible?" Robin agreed that the second formulation was more accurate but quickly added that she was still upset.

Then I asked her: "If your brother did sue you, what's the worst thing that could happen?" Robin first said that she was afraid of going to court against him, that he was a "powerful" person, that she might not know what to say, that he would intimidate her. I asked again, "What would be the worst thing—not knowing what to say or his trying to intimidate you?" As Robin explained, I kept repeating the same question, "What would be the worst thing . . ."

The longer my persistent and rather boring line of questioning continued, the less upset Robin felt and the more she realized that indeed there were far, far worse possible things that could have happened and that she definitely could "handle" this one. Finally we got to the point that the worst thing she could think of was that she might actually get dragged to court, lose, and have to get a second mortgage to pay her brother back. She also worried that it might be in the newspaper and she might be embarrassed to have people know about it.

We then talked about the differences between the two ways of thinking about the same event—hers and mine. I asked Robin to go over the differences in her mind each day at home. When we next met, she wasn't happy about the possibility that her brother might actually take her to court, but she wasn't paralyzed by worry and anger, either. Her new way of thinking about it took the edge off her upset.

Action Steps to Cut Down on the Anger in Your Life

Only recently in evolutionary time has our species evolved from primates whose lives are governed by raw emotion. That's why most of us still experience anger more often than we would like to.

Yoda was right. Fear does lead to anger, anger does lead to hate, and hate definitely leads to suffering. What follows is a brief list of questions to ask yourself and things to remember that I believe will help you to reduce the role of anger in your lives and in your sibling relationships.

- Is holding on to this anger really helping me?
- Do I feel that the anger somehow gives me power? Is there another way to get that power?
- When I'm angry, am I proud of myself for feeling and acting this way?

- Would I want my children to feel and act this way toward each other? If the same events that led to this resentment between me and my sibling occurred among my children, would I want this sort of resentment to linger?
- How will I feel about myself in the future if I get angry now?
- When I look back, what will I wish I had done?
- Would I want to be treated this way?
- What are the costs and the benefits of holding a grudge?

If these questions don't help you reduce your anger, and if you still find yourself frequently angry or walking around with a low level of anger all the time, something is wrong; you may want to consider the option of seeking a consultation with a professional.

Chapter 9

Understanding and Helping a Sibling with Mood Problems

Feelings are transient states: we feel happy, sad, scared, nervous, and usually these feelings pass. When feelings get stuck, they turn into moods. Negative moods are like stormy weather systems that stall and won't move out to sea. And, like storms, they bring unpleasantness with them.

If your sibling is persistently unhappy, irritable, or if her moods change unpredictably, two things are true. The first, as you well know, is that she's difficult to be around. The second is that she may have a primary or secondary mood disorder. And what you may not realize is that your moods and your sibling's moods are affecting how you see, think about, and respond to each other all the time in more ways than you might think.

Is My Sibling Depressed?

Before labeling your unhappy sibling as depressed, it's important to understand the many faces of depression.

Last month I met Bill, a middle-aged man who had been laid off from his long-standing job six weeks earlier. Since then, he hadn't felt like playing golf or going out to dinner, two of his favorite activities. His store of energy depleted; he spent much of his time worrying about his situation.

Frank, a much younger man with a high-paying job he enjoyed and an active social life, woke up one morning eight weeks ago overwhelmingly depressed. He slept all day and suffered from insomnia at night; he had little energy, felt agitated, and couldn't concentrate. Most concerning, he had active suicidal thoughts.

Both of these men described themselves as "depressed," as did their siblings, the older man's wife, and the younger man's partner. But beyond that diagnostic label, these men were more different than similar. To a psychologist or a psychiatrist, Bill's depression is mild; Frank's depression is severe.

Bill's depression was a reaction to a specific event—things he could identify, talk about, fret over, and ultimately figure out. Our discussions always have a practical slant. How should he best plan for what might happen? What kind of severance package can he expect? What would be the best time to consult a headhunter? They also have an emotionally supportive slant—recognizing that he had the rug pulled out from under his feet; the feeling of betrayal after his many years with the company. Both of these kinds of issues are things that he is able to talk about with both his brothers and his wife. His "therapy," in both the narrow sense of being in my office and in the wider sense of the many therapeutic and helpful discussions he has with family and friends, is common-sense based. It also reflects the fact that the depressed mood he has been experiencing for the past month is something that his family members can relate to as not so different from things they've been through. As a result, they can be concerned, but not anxious; supportive, but not pushy.

Although he's clearly very unhappy, Bill's depression would not be considered a "major depressive episode" by most psychologists and psychiatrists because he has only three symptoms of depression: sadness, low energy, and loss of pleasure in things he used to enjoy. His worry about the future is understandable given the realities of his situation. In the jargon of the day, he has an "adjustment disorder with mixed emotional features" (anxious and depressed mood).

On the other hand, Frank's symptoms, especially his inability to go to work, seemingly came from out of nowhere. For his family and friends, the biggest challenge was understanding what he was going through. Unlike Bill, he had no "real-world" complaints. He couldn't explain how he was feeling—he just felt terribly low, despairing, and overwhelmed by negative thoughts, none of which had anything to do with the realities of his day-to-day life and everything to do with his depression. That is, he wasn't upset about work, money, or relationships; instead, he was preoccupied by thoughts of death and dying.

But depression comes in other guises as well. Stacie, for example, described her younger sister Lora as short-tempered, rigid, negative, and irritable. Her first response to any suggestion was usually "No!" And she considered any alternative suggestion an insult.

What was not evident to Stacie—because Lora never cried, looked mad or sad, or talked about how badly she felt—was that Lora was self-doubting, discouraged about her career, pessimistic about the future and terribly unhappy in the present. When I met with Lora, she acknowledged that once in a while she cried "for no reason." Appearances notwithstanding, Lora was carrying anxiety and depression with her all the time. Despite the fact that she didn't identify it that way herself, Lora's depression was very real. In fact, she couldn't recall ever feeling otherwise.

Unlike either of the two men I've just described, Lora lacked a nondistressed frame of reference. She had felt this way as long as she could remember, and so truly didn't know that there was any other way to feel. She never would have sought psychological help on her own and would have been insulted if Stacie had suggested that she do so.

What Is Depression?

I've gone into detail about Frank, Bill, and Lora to illustrate how very different depression can look in different people and how a person can be both anxious and depressed at the same time. At one extreme, your sibling may be so obviously emotionally distraught and impaired that it frightens you. At the other extreme, your sibling may not even know herself that she is depressed may not even recognize it as depression for quite a while.

Depression isn't restricted to just one aspect of life: it is pervasive. Depressed people feel alone with their depression; they are convinced that nobody truly understands what they're going through.

If your sibling is depressed, she may:

- be self-critical
- cry frequently
- talk about suicide
- have no energy
- refrain from socializing and exercise
- eat and sleep too much or too little
- feel as if the weight of the world is on her shoulders
- have nothing to look forward to

What to Do If Your Sibling Is Depressed

If your brother or sister experiences depressed moods of whatever kind, it is a certainty that they will affect you. You'll probably have two reactions: first, a desire to help; second, you'll probably feel frustrated and begin to distance yourself from your sibling if your efforts fail, or if she rejects your offer.

Remember that depression is a cause as well as an effect. Depression is the result of neurochemical imbalances (insufficiencies), or negative life events, or both. Depression is also a cause of other changes in your sibling's life. Being depressed changes how your brother or sister reacts to events, to other people, to offers of help, and to even very good and sensible suggestions.

Before trying to help your sibling, you should try to determine if the depression is mild or severe. You can do this by asking three related questions:

- Can he or she identify an event or even a series of events that triggered the depression?
- How long has he or she been depressed?
- Is he or she able to function?

If your sibling has had a depressed mood for less than two weeks, can tell you what he is depressed about, and can still function, although perhaps not firing on all cylinders, his depressed mood is mild. He may be sad, may find himself on the verge of tears from time to time, and may feel less energetic than usual, but it's all a reaction to something that has happened or perhaps to something that he anticipates will happen soon. At the same time, he is able to look forward to a time when his problem will be resolved and his mood will return to normal.

Does My Sibling Have an Adjustment Disorder?

An adjustment disorder with depressed mood, or with "mixed emotional features" (what Bill had) is the key feature of this type of disorder. The depression is triggered by a specific event—the loss of a job, a divorce, a child leaving for college. In these cases, your sibling needs time to "adjust" to his change in circumstances. Even if your sibling's symptoms worsen to include hopelessness, it would still be characterized as an adjustment disorder.

Another key feature of an adjustment disorder is that you are able to identify with your sibling's emotional distress. If you find yourself thinking, "I'd be upset, too, if I was going through that," then your sibling probably has an adjustment disorder.

Sometimes the depressed mood is so mild that it resolves itself with support from you and other family and friends and with the resolution of the problem that set it off. If the depressed mood lingers or if it starts to interfere with his ability to take action that would help resolve the problem, your sibling will probably benefit from finding a professional to talk to about his concerns. This need not be a long-term undertaking. People are often helped a great deal from just a few meetings.

One technique that I use, and you can try if your sibling's depression is mild and infrequent, is to ask your sibling to make a list of the activities that she enjoys. Typically, the list is short. But if you persevere, your sibling will probably be able to list a few. Then, encourage her to try one of these when she feels low. Very often, depressed people are surprised to find that the activity is enjoyable after all and that they've had a respite from their very low mood swing.

Is My Sibling Seriously Depressed?

A person who is seriously depressed

- doesn't feel like getting up in the morning
- wakes in the middle of the night with terrible thoughts
- doesn't eat or sleep well
- has symptoms that last for more than a few weeks
- may have thoughts of death or suicide
- sees the future as bleak and can't imagine things getting better

Some seriously depressed people can't identify anything about which they are depressed. They say things like, "Everything is fine. I have a great family. I like my job. I'm making enough money. I'm healthy. I just feel like I weigh a thousand pounds and keep thinking about killing myself."

At this point, seeking professional help is a necessity. If your brother or sister refuses to consult a psychologist or a psychiatrist, you should encourage him or her to talk with a physician who may prescribe one of the newer antidepressants and may also be able to convince him or her to give therapy a try.

Does My Sibling Have a Mood Disorder?

In between the extremes of people who have very mildly depressed moods and those who are profoundly depressed are people who experience depressed or anxious moods, or a combination of these, most of the time, or all of the time, but at a more moderate level. Everything they say and do is colored by these difficulties with mood regulation.

The problems of people in this third group may not meet diagnostic criteria for major depression or anxiety disorder. This does not mean that their problems with mood are any less real. Life can be just as difficult for siblings with these milder mood problems as it is for those who have the more severe forms of mood disorder. Most important to our concerns in this book, it can be just as difficult for you to know how to respond to your anxious or depressed brother or sister. It may actually be more challenging, because you may not know, and your sibling may not know, that the problem exists.

If your sibling is frequently depressed or if his depression is more severe, your practical advice is much less likely to be accepted—and even if it is accepted, it probably won't work. A depressed mood that lasts longer than a week or so, especially if it isn't a reaction to a specific stressful event, is probably not going to go away without some outside help.

Is My Sibling Anxious?

Anxiety is often harder to pin down than depression because it manifests itself in many ways. I've had many people say "no" when I've asked if they were worried, anxious, or upset and then acknowledged that they felt a great deal of "uncertainty," or a very high level of "concern." Some anxious people vehemently deny internal discomfort of any kind and attribute their nonstop activity to being "very busy." If your sibling is irritable, grumpy, negative, short-tempered, tense, or hypercritical most of the time, there's a good chance that he's anxious.

If your sibling is anxious, she may:

- appear agitated
- worry constantly
- have a tremor in her voice or a twitch in her eye
- have trouble sleeping
- startle easily
- worry about minor events
- be unable to quell her worries

The Many Faces of Anxiety

Mike, a retired salesman in his early sixties, spent much of his time traveling the world with his wife. After one spectacular trip, he returned home feeling uneasy. When his sister asked him what was wrong, he said, "I'm really stressed. We've been traveling a lot, and now I've got all this paperwork to catch up on, and we've got to make a decision about redoing the guest bedroom; it's just terrible." He wasn't kidding—he believed that his predicament was terrible.

Like Mike, most anxious people aren't aware of their anxiety. And those around them may not think of them as anxious. But they do remark on their irritability, grumpiness, or impatience. Some anxious people are very abrasive, the type who say, "I don't get migraines. I give other people migraines." The first step in helping your anxious sibling is to recognize the condition.

What Is Anxiety?

Anxiety has both physical and cognitive symptoms. People who are anxious often have three traits in common:

1. They worry excessively,
   - sometimes over real issues;
   - sometimes about issues over which they have no control, such as the likelihood that the sun may burn out in another hundred million years.

2. They experience physical symptoms that are hard to understand unless you've experienced them yourself. They feel jittery, as if they're jumping out of their skins, but, paradoxically, don't know that they're jittery because they've never felt otherwise. It's almost as if they've been drinking ten cups of very strong coffee every day for so many years that they don't remember what it was like before.

3. They aren't aware of their anxiety until they learn to overcome it.

The Blurry Line between Depression and Anxiety

At the extremes, the symptoms of depression and anxiety are obviously physiological and psychological. Most times, however, the signs are subtler. Often, symptoms overlap.

Researchers and personality theorists have long debated whether worry (anxiety) and sadness (depression) are two different emotions or two aspects of the same emotion. Many of the people I see have both problems. The sketch that follows shows how the symptoms of anxiety and depression are related in terms of emotional and physiological arousal (pulse, respiration rate, blood pressure, and adrenaline level), and one's perception of mood as positive or negative. When your sibling is in a state of low arousal and a positive mood, she would probably describe herself as "relaxed." When she is in a state of moderately low arousal with a negative mood, she probably describes herself as sad. But if her level of arousal is very low and her mood is very negative, she is depressed. On the other hand, if her arousal level is high and her mood is positive, she's excited. If arousal is high and mood is very negative, she is both anxious and depressed.

	negative mood	positive mood
high emotional arousal	depression and anxiety	excitement
low emotional arousal	depression	calm and relaxed

Is My Sibling Irritable and Irritating?

Your sibling may have mood problems that fall far short of being major depression yet that still affect her daily functioning and especially her interactions with family members. Millions of people experience low levels of depression every day, usually characterized by negativity, irritability, and grumpiness. One of the major reasons these conditions aren't more widely recognized is because people with mild mood problems often don't realize it themselves. They may have always felt that way, and so don't know there is any other way to feel. The mood difficulties may have been with them for so long that they have incorporated them into the way they think of themselves. I've met many people who typically describe their mood as "okay," when what they are really experiencing is a chronic, low-level depression. For them the world is always tinged with gray. It's very hard for them to enjoy life's small pleasures: a dogwood tree in bloom, a picturesque scene, a sunset. Only life's big events—taking an exotic trip, buying an expensive car, becoming hugely successful at work—seem to make an impression on them. And then, these may only cut through their mood once; the next exotic vacation won't pack the same punch.

On the interpersonal front, people who walk around in a chronically depressed mood tend to have something negative to say about almost anything. They may have learned to pretend to be upbeat in some social situations and some can pretend very well indeed. But when around family, the negative almost always comes out in full force. I was present at the following brief exchange between a chronically but mildly depressed man and his more upbeat sibling:

"Isn't it a beautiful day?"

"Yeah, it's nice now, but I don't trust it."

Such a response would be laughable were it not so sad. The brother for whom the glass was always half empty didn't think of himself as depressed and would have been offended if his upbeat brother had suggested that he was. It wasn't his fault if he saw life the way it was—basically miserable. He wasn't suicidal, never cried, always got out of bed and went to work. He was, in a word, "fine."

Unfortunately, there isn't much you can do to help your chronically depressed sibling unless he or she wants to be helped. Medication and therapy are effective treatments for depression, but they only work if people are ready to acknowledge the problem and seek its alleviation.

Is My Sibling Too Dependent?

Gail's brother had been depressed for as long as she could re-member. She recommended that he get some therapy but balked when he asked her to go with him. Gail told me that her brother's agenda was not to drag her into therapy in order to blame her for all his life's difficulties. It was, rather, to lean on her at a time when he was feeling inadequate and alone. Gail accompanied him to a psychologist for two or three visits, feeling that she had done enough to help him get started. Theoretically, she was absolutely right. In fact, however, her brother needed more than she had to offer. He soon dropped out of therapy, saying he would return only if she went with him.

I advised Gail to continue accompanying her brother to therapy as long as she was able. Sure, he was being extremely dependent, but I urged her to think of him as if he were a person who was recovering from a heart attack and needed extra accommodation.

Gail didn't agree. She said that she knew she "should" go the extra mile for her brother but her schedule didn't allow her to.

The choice facing Gail was whether to rely on constructive or destructive entitlement. If she chose constructive entitlement, she would have welcomed the opportunity to be of real help to her brother as a way of increasing her feeling of her own self-worth. Instead, she chose to rely on destructive entitlement, thinking about how much she had already done for him and how busy she was. None of this was mean-spirited; she expressed affection and concern for her brother. It was rather a failure to truly appreciate the opportunity with which she was presented.

Does My Sibling Have Bipolar Disorder?

Like depression and anxiety, bipolar disorder can be wild and unmistakable or subtle and very hard to distinguish from garden-variety moodiness. The older term for this illness, manic-depressive psychosis, better captured the reality of the illness in its more severe forms, which can involve periods of profound depression and suicidal thoughts alternating with periods of euphoric elation and almost unbelievable grandiose thinking. A person with a very mild bipolar disorder may be chronically irritable and is usually seen by relatives and friends as emotionally very intense, sometimes without apparent reason. He may also sometimes become so fired up by an idea or a project that he can go twenty-four or more hours without sleep.

This does not mean that if your sister stays up all night wrapping Christmas gifts, she has bipolar disorder and should see a psychiatrist or needs medication. Neither does it mean that your irritable and grumpy older brother deserves this diagnosis. It does mean that if your brother or sister regularly suffers from unpredictable emotional ups and downs, you may suggest that he or she consult a psychologist or a psychiatrist with expertise in this area who can provide guidance about treatment options.

Does My Sibling Suffer from Alcoholism and/or Substance Abuse?

Hundreds of books have been written about the problem of alcohol and substance abuse and its treatment. If you have a sibling who is heavily alcohol or drug dependent, it's worth learning as much as you can. Two good places to start are the web sites of the National Institute of Drug Abuse (www.nida.nih.gov) and the National Institute of Alcoholism and Alcohol Abuse (www.niaaa.nih.gov), where you'll find up-to-date information on current research and new treatments.

One of the things that mystifies many family members is how a person can continue to drink or use drugs when it is so clearly hurting them in so many ways. The short answer is that drug abuse and alcoholism are compulsive diseases of the brain. Drugs and alcohol affect brain functioning in two separate but related ways. They activate reward centers, leading to the euphoria, disinhibition, and other "altered states" that drug and alcohol abusers are seeking. At the same time, these substances affect the prefrontal cortex, the part of the brain responsible for executive functioning: planning, considering long-term consequences, and making rational decisions. This is why a man can decide to have only one drink at a party and after that one drink think that a second drink is not such a bad idea after all. It is also why he can keep drinking long after it has become clear to all that he is damaging his liver and shortening his life.

Because of the dual brain effects of these substances, treatment is difficult and long. People with this disease may not get better after one or even two stays in a treatment setting. It's not uncommon for a recovering alcoholic to say something like, "The first four rehabs I went to didn't do anything for me; the fifth one was really good. They knew what they were doing and it helped me stop drinking." The truth is probably that each of them helped and it was their cumulative effect that led to the cessation of the drinking.

If you and your family are confronted with the problem of an alcoholic or a sibling who abuses another substance, you must be prepared for a long, long haul. One of the best things you can do is to find resources and support that will help you stay emotionally healthy through it all, whether your sibling recovers or not. I strongly recommend that you look into the various support groups in your area for relatives of alcoholics and drug abusers. In addition to providing emotional support, these groups can give you specific advice, helpful strategies, and information about treatment facilities. If you try a group and it doesn't feel right, find another—there are so many options today that you're sure to find one where you'll feel comfortable.

Does My Sibling Need Professional Help?

Some of the mood problems described above resolve themselves over time, with or without the emotional support of caring friends and family. Major depression, bipolar disorder, and substance abuse of the sort that you've just read about are not in this category.

Siblings coping with these types of issues will need professional help. With few exceptions, he (your brother) will need to be coaxed, cajoled, and encouraged to seek and accept that help. She (your sister) may accept your recommendation more quickly and may even seek help on her own. This is not sexist stereotyping; it's an observation that all mental health professionals share, and one you should be aware of.

Action Steps to Help a Depressed or Anxious Brother or Sister Seek Help

If you had a very solid relationship with your sibling before his depression started, you probably can and should go ahead and directly suggest that he get some professional help.

If, however, your relationship with the sibling in question isn't very close and comfortable, you run the risk that such a recommendation may be perceived as insulting or pushy. In this case, don't get drawn into mutual grumpiness. Don't respond to each of his or her complaints with a complaint of your own, such as, "What's the matter with you? Every word out of your mouth is nasty! You ought to see a psychiatrist!" Your suggesting it won't make a difference until you first establish your trustworthiness. After that, you may be able to find a way to make the suggestion more appealing and convincing.

Here are some strategies that will help you open a conversation:

• Express concern, but do not advise. Almost anybody will accept a brother or a sister's nonjudgmental concern expressed simply and fairly directly, such as, "I'm concerned about you. How are you feeling?" Your brother or your sister may take the opportunity to talk forthrightly with you, perhaps adding that they hadn't wanted to say anything because they were not sure you wanted to hear it. Your brother or sister may also try to reassure you that there's no reason for your concern. It's extraordinarily unlikely that your sibling will be angry.

• Share an observation, such as:
  • "I've noticed that things have been getting to you lately."
  • "That's the second or third time you've said, 'If I live that long.' Is everything all right?"
  • "You seem to be out of sorts (down on yourself) lately and I'm concerned."

By asking your questions, you may help your sibling acknowledge that she is, and has been, depressed or anxious and needs psychological counseling. It's possible that she has already done so, in which case your concern will be especially appreciated. Of course, it's possible that she may be offended anyway. Unfortunately, many people still feel that seeking psychological help is stigmatizing.

• Talk about yourself instead. Your sibling may be more comfortable if you first acknowledge that you have experienced anxious or depressed moods, too. Start with a self-revealing statement such as, "You know, last year when I had all that trouble at work I was really depressed for about six months." This statement by itself may be enough to get a conversation moving. If you were in therapy or took medication for a period of time and found that it helped you, talking about this can be a powerful way to show that you are concerned and that help is available.

· If you know that your brother will not be interested in talking about his feelings with you or some "shrink," suggest that he see his family doctor. You can say something like, "You've been looking so tired lately; have you talked to your doctor?"

· Don't assume that your sibling knows what he's feeling, or why. I've seen a surprising number of people who are aware of their anger but not of their depression or are tuned into all the little things that bother them but not to the level of anxiety that makes it so easy for small things to drive them nuts.

· Look for opportunities to build up your storehouse of constructive entitlement. Learn to rely on it more and more. Welcome opportunities to lend a hand to a depressed brother or sister.

· Don't worry about being enabling. Instead, look for ways to be ennobling.

· Expect to encounter frustration. Many people, especially men, are reluctant to seek help. They will probably counter your suggestion by saying, "Leave me alone, I'll work it out myself." When this happens, remember Winston Churchills' exhortation: "Never give up, never, never, never . . ."

· Above all, remember that your sibling's emotional difficulties are not directed at you. They upset him or her at least as much as they do you, and probably a great deal more. They are doubtless annoying at times, demanding at times, and grumpy at times, but the annoying quality and grumpiness come from their inner distress. It may seem that they're doing things to get at you, but this is not likely to be so. If they were aware of how their behavior puts you off, they would feel bad about it and stop it if they could.

The people you'll read about in the next chapter, by way of contrast, for the most part don't give a damn about you or how their actions affect you. The reason I've written two longish chapters about these two categories of "difficult" siblings can be summed up in one sentence: know the difference between a distressed sibling and a nasty one; do everything you can to help the former and be careful of the latter.

Chapter 10

Understanding and Managing Your Sibling's Difficult Personality

"You look just like sisters." People make comments like that all the time, implying an expectation that siblings share many traits. And, in fact, siblings often do share many features: body type, intelligence, overall appearance, hair and eye color, and various abilities, whether in music, the arts, or athletics. But when it comes to what we commonly call "personality," there are often more differences than similarities.

What Is Personality?

Each person has a relatively consistent way of perceiving, feeling, and responding to people and events. These ways of perceiving, feeling, and responding may, of course, vary to a certain extent from one situation to another; a person may be quiet among new acquaintances and more energetic among old friends, or upbeat and enthusiastic at work but withdrawn and morose when alone.

These relatively stable characteristics comprise the core of a person's personality. Personalities can differ radically among siblings, probably because the combination of genetic and learned factors is so much more complicated than it is for the physical traits I just listed. One of the challenges involved in healing a relationship with a brother or a sister is learning to accept and appreciate these personality differences.

Character: The Other Side of Personality

There's another aspect to personality, though, which psychologists in the first half of the past century called character. In 1937, the renowned psychologist Gordon Allport wrote, "Character enters the situation only when this personal effort is judged from the standpoint of some code. Character is personality evaluated and personality is character devaluated."

This second side of personality reflects the extent to which a person is able and willing to shape his behavior so that it is moral. Some personality characteristics may be harder to harness in this way, but none makes immoral behavior a necessity. For example, your brother may be impulsive, but as long as he channels and controls his impulsivity, he can behave in moral ways so that he doesn't hurt anybody. On the other hand, he can allow his impulsivity to rule him, and as a result will cause real and lasting pain. My point is that being impulsive doesn't define anyone. What counts is how one handles the impulsivity.

This chapter will explore ways to deal with siblings who do not choose to use their personality for good but rather to in some way advance what they believe is their interests. That they are often mistaken in what is truly in their interests only adds to the pain that this sort of immoral and amoral behavior causes.

In other words, the previous chapters in this book dealt with the larger category of people who have generally good intentions and sometimes make mistakes. In this chapter, we'll consider siblings who hurt others with no regrets.

A Cautionary Note

It is a truism among mental health professionals that the healthier and psychologically stronger person in a relationship is almost always the one who seeks therapy and who actively looks for change. What you will read in this chapter is intended to give you some tools that will help you to better understand your difficult brother or sister. I believe that this information and quasi-diagnostic material has the potential to be genuinely useful; I wouldn't have included it otherwise. It also has the potential to be damaging, and it is that potential that I want to address here. It's important, for example, not to use this information to blame, unfairly criticize, or put your sibling down.

I've already addressed the very great danger involved in gossip, especially gossip of the character-assassinating variety. The temptation to do so may be great, especially when your sibling is at his or her worst, but giving in to that temptation will not help. Remember that character assassination, like gossip, can rebound. After the verbal bullets wound or destroy the other person, they ricochet around until they finally come back to strike you. The damage done to your character will be as real as the damage done to the person with whom you are angry, in neither case will it be easily undone.

People Who Use People

Some people—and we've all met them—routinely treat others as objects. Many of them have extraordinary interpersonal skills. The problem lies in the fact that they don't put these skills to work in the service of achieving close and mutually supportive relationships, but, rather, they use them to advance their personal interests. That they are often mistaken in what is truly in their interests only adds to the pain that this sort of immoral and amoral behavior causes.

Figuring out how to handle someone like this is a real challenge. Many times, the best solution is to find a way around the problem.

Marsha, for example, described her brother Alfie as unbelievably charming. A skillful and facile liar, he knew exactly how to manipulate people to get what he wanted. Even when caught in a lie, he never seemed at a loss for words, never was embarrassed or awkward. "It's as if lying comes more naturally to him than the truth," Marsha said. "It doesn't seem to take any effort or worry." He never did anything unless it had a clear, immediate, and material benefit for him.

If she tried avoiding him, she felt guilty, but watching him operate at close range made her blood boil. When she tried to tell him how distressing she found his actions, he "explained" his actions in a way that made them sound reasonable.

At the same time, Alfie relied on Marsha's good nature and affection to keep her from telling people the truth about him, and it had always worked. When she thought of telling people of his untrustworthiness, Marsha anticipated feeling very guilty. When she played along with his game, she felt equally guilty. She was at a loss as to how to deal with him.

What to Do

I suggested that she find a circumspect way to communicate to others her reservations about her brother rather than attacking him broadside. If, for instance, her cousin called to say, "Alfie is going to get me a great deal on a used BMW," Marsha could reply, "I understand that the local dealer has some great prices and they give extended warranties, too." In this way, Marsha is conveying her reservation about Alfie's offer by not showing enthusiasm for it, and is offering an alternative in its place. But notice—she's not saying anything negative about her brother.

People Who Think of Only Themselves

Other people are overly concerned with themselves, to the exclusion of others. They tend to find it extraordinarily tempting to view events from only one perspective: how those events affect them.

When Mike cornered his younger brother for a heart-to-heart talk in which he shared all his pent-up hostility, all he could think about was how great it felt to get all of this off his chest, how proud he was of himself for being open and honest, for sharing his innermost feelings. He didn't think for a moment of how what he said might affect his brother. He didn't consider anything except how he was feeling.

Other people don't consider the perspectives of others because they think of other people as extensions of themselves. For example, Brendon was emotionally and materially stingy with his brother, sister, parents and children, coworkers and subordinates. Toward them, he was quick to react to any real or imagined affront and could hold a grudge for decades. Many people saw him as the prototypical "What's in it for me?" man. Toward his girlfriend Sheila, however, he was generous, tolerant, willing to accept criticism, and admiring. How could this be so? It was because he didn't see Sheila as a unique human being, either, but rather as an extension of himself. So buying Sheila a new car was really buying himself a new car; laughing at Sheila's joke was laughing at his own joke; praising Sheila's skill on the golf course was akin to bragging about his own skill.

What to Do

If your sibling doesn't seem to care about you or those close to you, the best thing you can do is to realize that this is a result of their personality, not your unlovableness. In other words, you have to accept that there are people who can love only one person at a time, or who can't love anyone except as a reflection of themselves. Nothing you can do will change this. Instead, do whatever you can to change and lower your expectations. And practice a new mantra: "This isn't about me."

People Who Need to Be Adored

Some difficult siblings demand that those in their family adore, admire, and worship them. Obviously, those having this need find it difficult to create meaningful reciprocal relationships.

Take Ben's brother Sam who, although successful and respected at work, was emotionally very needy. He had an almost insatiable need to be admired and looked up to. His younger sister Alix did so, and all was well between them. Ben, however, looked on Sam as an equal, which meant that he'd occasionally challenge one of Sam's pronouncements. Sam couldn't tolerate such a challenge, and grew emotionally stingy toward Ben, blaming him for many situations beyond Ben's control.

This left Ben very confused. He felt as if he were a perpetual disappointment to Sam, and couldn't understand what was wrong with him and why he couldn't get along with his brother. And since Sam and Alix had such a good relationship, Ben naturally concluded that he was to blame for the brothers' inability to get along with each other.

But in my view, Ben wasn't doing anything wrong. Sam is the kind of sibling who, wrapped up in narcissistic needs, requires constant adulation. He says things with the sole intent of making himself look or feel better than the person to whom he's speaking. He may be infuriatingly unconcerned about having inconvenienced anyone. Yet he is capable of feeling remorse, even if he fights those feelings. All Ben has to realize is that his role in life isn't to support his brother's narcissistic habit.

Here are some tips for dealing with siblings who need to be adored:

- Don't overgive. It's sometimes tempting to flatter or do whatever they want in the hope that they will eventually reciprocate. This is unlikely to work and quite likely to lead you to becoming resentful.
- Don't withhold, either. Another temptation when dealing with siblings who so clearly need to be admired is to refuse to admire or respond positively to anything. Rather then effusive praise or backlash withholding, let yourself say something positive—just as you would if he wasn't your sibling.
- Be open to change but don't expect it. Although this particular difficult sibling is more benign than some, he's no more likely to change than those with more serious personality problems.

The Bully

When we think of bullies, we think of children in a schoolyard. But bullies grow up, and if they are our siblings, we have to learn to deal with them as adults.

Brad, whom many nonprofessionals (and some professionals as well) would classify as having OPD, or "obnoxious personality disorder," enjoyed the feeling of power and control he had, the ability to intimidate others and to make them do what he wanted because they were afraid of him. His motto was, "Do unto others before they get a chance to do unto you." He was very quick to think that other people were criticizing him and equally quick to react angrily or to counterattack; he also tended to hold a grudge for a long time. He did not seem to feel any remorse about having frightened or hurt other people. He was either unwilling or unable to recognize or appreciate other people's feelings and emotional needs. His confrontations with his brothers were often aggressive, both verbally and physically. If things didn't go his way, he yelled, slammed doors, pushed, and generally used his size to intimidate. He liked the feeling he got when he was angry with someone, and saw nothing wrong with using his anger in that way. To the best of my knowledge, he had never beaten anybody up but he had punched holes in walls when angry and was once arrested for threatening the driver of another car with a handgun. If he ever lost a minute's sleep over anything he'd done that hurt or frightened somebody, nobody in his family knew about it.

What to Do

People like Brad need very clear boundaries that distinguish between acceptable and unacceptable behavior. Telling them that they're hurting your feelings won't help—that's their goal. Like aggressive children and adolescents, they need to know that inappropriate behavior will have clear and meaningful consequences. Unfortunately, it's not as simple as taking away television privileges or grounding them.

I believe that bullies like Brad should be told that they cannot act out in your presence and if they do, they will not be welcomed. You can say something like, "I can't permit this sort of behavior in my home; if you can't control yourself, you won't be invited back." If the bullying becomes physically aggressive, then say that you will call the local police department. Obviously you don't want to file an assault charge against your brother, but if you are prepared to do so if it's needed, and if he believes that you're ready to do so, it will help him remember to control himself.

The Con Artist

Alex was a different type of bully—he had no problem with his social skills. He was a terrifically successful salesman, whether it involved selling stocks and bonds, exotic cars, or himself. People he met in business or socially enjoyed his company; he was not just liked, but well liked. Yet he routinely took advantage of people. And after he did, he suffered no pangs of conscience. His stomach didn't churn after a heated encounter, nor did his palms sweat with the fear that he'd be caught in a lie. If he ever felt any guilt over having taken advantage of people who trusted him, the guilt was minor and fleeting. Alex was neither conflicted nor concerned.

As psychologist David Shapiro points out in his book *Neurotic Styles,* successful con artists and criminals often are very skillful in sizing up people and situations and rely on this skill in their daily activities. They are often geniuses at intuiting people's hopes and fantasies, and their vulnerabilities. It seems as if people with this quality should also be empathetic, because they are able to understand what the other person is likely to feel and how the other person is likely to respond. But this ability has nothing to do with real empathy.

The difference is that the con artist puts his empathic understanding to work in only one way: to reach his goal. Not to help anybody else, not to support anybody through a crisis, but for his own purposes. David Shapiro describes this type of psychopath this way: "He is . . . not so much interested in what is said to him as in the possibilities the situation offers. He is, and consciously so, not so much interested in what he says as in how well it works."

Con artists and other criminals are but extreme examples of psychopaths. When you confront your sister about a blatant lie she told you a month ago and she responds, "I'm sure I believed it when I said it," she, too, is revealing a psychopathic style. When she lies as easily as another person would fall off a horse, she's revealing a psychopathic style. When she apologizes and vows to do better with absolutely no real intention of changing at all, she's revealing a psychopathic style.

As different as they are, Alex and Brad share several traits. They both view people as objects rather than as full human beings in their own right. They are also extremely unlikely to request psychological help to change their nature. They may seek services for a specific problem such as insomnia, weight loss, relief of anxiety, or smoking cessation, but not for personality change.

They also are convinced that anything that goes wrong is somebody else's fault, not theirs. This is the fundamental difference between the Alex's of the world and the other difficult siblings you've read about in other chapters of this book. Most of these other men and women are, on occasion, able to recognize that they may just possibly have contributed ever so slightly to friction between themselves and you. They all are able to apologize for an outburst, although they may not do it very often. And, most important, they are able to think about what they can do to improve a relationship. Brad and Alex and others like them think only about how they can get you to do what they want; it's the person as object all over again.

What to Do

If there's an Alex in your life, and if you are essentially a trusting person, you will need to learn to be less trusting—not in general, but toward that sibling. Though I usually counsel people to give everyone the benefit of the doubt, I also know that those who do can put themselves at risk by believing those who shouldn't be trusted. If you discover that your sister has strong psychopathic tendencies, don't believe everything she says. Don't assume that she's always lying, but seriously consider the possibility that she may be.

The Splitter

Some people make themselves feel important by intruding in and mucking around in other people's relationships. In that these people often end up dividing people, we refer to them as "splitters." The splitter's machinations often have a passive-aggressive quality: many times, splitters defend themselves by saying, "I'm just trying to help."

This is one of the more difficult kinds of annoying behaviors to counter. How can you blame them for the inconvenience, discomfort, or embarrassment they caused you if they claim they were only trying to help?

People who resort to this type of comment are sometimes referred to as having passive-aggressive personalities. Unlike some psychological jargon, this term actually means what it seems it should: it refers to people who are actually being aggressive but do so in an indirect way. Forgetting an appointment or an obligation is an example of manifesting one's anger or aggression passively. "I'm sorry, I'm so forgetful," is the passive-aggressive analog to the more blatantly aggressive, "That was the dumbest idea I've heard all month, I'll be damned if I'm going to do it."

But to deal with a splitter, you need to pay attention to the effects of his actions, not his intentions. Amelia, for example, worked very hard to get her relationship with her father to be as good as it was. He was an extraordinarily difficult man with many personality quirks of his own. Despite this, she invited her father over at least once a month, encouraged him to attend every family event and as many of the children's school and extracurricular activities as possible, and told him to feel free to come over unannounced anytime.

Yet her younger sister and older brother regularly told her that they thought it was "a shame" that her relationship with their father was not better than it was. They told her that he had confided in them that the real reason he so infrequently visited her, despite living less than an hour away, was that he "didn't feel comfortable" in her home. And they never offered any concrete suggestions as to what she might do to change her relationship with her father.

On the surface, Amelia's siblings' comments were sympathetic, but their real intent was nasty. They each implied that they had a better relationship with their father than Amelia did. And if Amelia had confronted them with their nastiness, her sister and her brother would have reacted in surprise: "But we were only trying to help!" This is the essence of passive-aggressive behavior. It also demonstrates the type of splitting behavior that drives a wedge between two people.

What to Do

Confronting such behavior angrily never works. The best response to passive aggression is to express gratitude.

If you are in a situation like Amelia's, tell your sibling how much you appreciate her expression of caring and concern. If she genuinely meant to be helpful, this is the appropriate recognition. If, on the other hand, her sub rosa intention was to make you feel bad about yourself or something you did or did not do, you will have very politely spoiled it for her. And there is a possibility that by dealing with the behavior in this way, your sibling may eventually change.

Air Your Laundry in Public

Here's another suggestion—go public. Amelia, for instance, casually mentioned at a family gathering how her siblings had been so helpful in letting her know that her father didn't feel welcome at her house. "What can I do?" she asked him. He then had the chance to clarify his position: he wasn't used to just dropping in and would rather she invite him for a specific time so that he knew he was expected. When her siblings told her later that they were shocked and embarrassed that she had said that, she told them that she was "just trying to be helpful."

Here are more suggestions for dealing with a passive-aggressive sibling:

• If your sibling "forgets" to get back to you about an event, call or send a polite follow-up postcard saying that you haven't heard and so assume he or she won't be attending and ask him or her to let you know if this isn't correct.

• If your sibling has been proven to be unreliable in the past, make sure you have backup. If he doesn't show up, you'll not be stuck, and if he does, there will be extra hands.

• If your sibling likes to tell you what other people think of you, thank him for the information and let him know that you'll take it up with the other person. Then, ask the person if the statement is true.

Extraordinary Selfishness

Another type of difficult sibling is one whose selfishness seems boundless. Woody was slowly dying of prostate cancer. He had no close relatives except for his two children, Larry and Beth. Beth dropped everything to be with him as the end approached and was astonished to find that her brother was unwilling to do the same. It was not only the additional burden of being the only caretaker that upset her, it was the additional blow of being confronted by such blatant unfairness. She couldn't believe that Larry could be so heartless toward both herself and their father.

Beth was well aware that the relationship between father and son had never been very good—that her father could be, in fact often was, critical, impatient, controlling, and unpleasant. She had observed many instances of meanness by her father directed toward her brother, some of which were upsetting to her even to witness. Even with all this as backdrop, she could still not come to grips with the cavalier way in which her brother refused to assist her as she did what she could to make their father's last days comfortable. He was too busy, he insisted. They had never been close, he reminded her. He would come later, when he was really needed, closer to the end.

He did come, for two days, at the end of their father's life. He left before the funeral, and neglected to help with its planning. By the time Beth came to see me, she was deeply confused. Try as she might, she couldn't identify any reason for her brother's behavior. Neither could she relate to it in any personal way. Especially befuddling to her was the fact that her brother seemed unperturbed, while she was so upset that she asked her internist for medication so that she could sleep and work.

But her most pressing question was, "How could he be so heartless?" She also had a deeper question—one she was afraid to ask even herself—"If he is such an awful person, what does that say about our parents and what does it say about me?"

Part of the answer, I told Beth, was that her brother had the kind of destructive entitlement you read about in Chapter 7. It's possible that when Larry was young, unfairly high expectations were set for him. Or perhaps he knew at an early age that his sister was the favored child.

Still, it's hard to see how this level of destructive parentification could, by itself, account for such willfully uncaring behavior as Larry's. Life is full of examples of people who have experienced far worse injustices. After thinking about this conundrum for many years, I'm afraid that I still don't have a truly satisfactory explanation. I don't think that destructive entitlement by itself explains the whole story because it doesn't account for the fact that people can choose to reject the destructive entitlement they've accrued.

Part of the answer, David Shapiro and others suggest, may lie in the fact that some people are more impulsive than others, and are unable to reflect on the meanings and long-term consequences of their actions. As one young man recently said to me, "I remember what I did but I try not to think about it because it makes me feel bad." It did make him feel bad, but not very much and not for long enough to affect his future actions.

Destructive Entitlement in the Extreme

Some of the most difficult siblings are beset by a more malignant type of destructive entitlement than the one discussed in Chapter 7. In that chapter, we encountered siblings who are so caught up in their own lives that they are oblivious to what others need. Other siblings, however, are completely aware of your situation and decide to not care about you. Obviously, this is much more hurtful.

Adrienne was a very warm, natural, and unaffected woman of about forty with two small children and one very large dog. She and her husband were very busy professionals, their children were involved in sports and other activities, and their home was always busy and sometimes a bit disorganized. Nonetheless, when Zoe, Adrienne's oldest sister, said she'd like to come visit, Adrienne welcomed her warmly. Imagine her shock to discover that Zoe had used her computer to send a friend an e-mail in which she vigorously insulted Adrienne, her parenting, her professional accomplishments, and her children's behavior.

When You Come to a Dead End

If your sibling is more like Alex, Sam, and Brad, you may have to accept the fact that he or she may never change. For some siblings, a broken relationship cannot be mended until the person directly responsible for the fracture starts to make changes. Some people I've talked to become so worn down by their sibling's lack of humanity and decency that they want to cut off all communication, to live as if their sibling did not exist.

I understand this feeling, but I still suggest that you try to find an alternative to a total cutoff. In my experience, it's very hard for good people to take irrevocable actions without paying an emotional cost. The Alexs and Brads of this world have no second thoughts, worries, or regrets over their actions—but you do.

To spare yourself the anguish that would result from a complete estrangement, I suggest that you try to find a way to leave the door open for change while being realistic and taking appropriate precautions. You don't need to invite your brother to spend Christmas with you and you shouldn't invest in his latest real estate deal. But you can return a phone call if you get one. You can keep him on your Christmas card list. Those are small things but they should be enough to relieve you from any doubt that, "Maybe if I waited, he would have changed."

Try to Not Make Excuses

You may be tempted to make excuses for the difficult sibling. Your thinking may run this way: "If my sister is behaving this badly, it must mean that she was terribly hurt, in which case I should be understanding, patient, and accepting."

This kind of thinking is reinforced by the popularity of the various "recovery movements," just as it is by the current tendency to medicalize unpleasant and inconsiderate patterns of behavior. Many adults have recently been diagnosed with attention deficit disorder, for example.

However, excusing someone's chronic lateness or lack of responsibility on the basis of ADD or any other so-called impairment helps nobody. It doesn't help the person, because there is no pressure to change. It doesn't help the person's siblings or spouse, because the behavior continues unabated.

Compassion for the truly mentally ill is, of course, a very good thing. But the vast majority of those people who are inconsiderate and selfish are not mentally ill. Your obnoxious and uncaring brother or sister is extraordinarily unlikely to have instincts, urges, or feelings drastically different from yours or mine. It's true that they may feel some of these things more strongly than you do. They may live with some forms of psychological distress that you have been spared. They may have frequent headaches, acid reflux, or irritable bowel syndrome. They may experience high levels of anxiety—an important possibility which I discussed in the previous chapter. Any of these features and issues may make life difficult for your brother or your sister; they do not, however, excuse their behavior.

Remember—these siblings have never bothered to make the effort to counter their more base, selfish, and just plain nasty impulses. In a way, they're not that much different from the rest of humanity. At times, we are all selfish, stubborn, arrogant, mean-spirited, impatient, hypercritical, and blind to the needs of others. The difference is that most of us feel bad about these faults and at least once in a while try to do something about them. Most of us are willing to consider the possibility that we may be responsible for something that goes wrong between us and other people.

People with the kinds of personality problems that I've been describing are convinced that all problems are somebody else's fault. If there is a misunderstanding, it's always the other person's fault. One woman with whom I talked told me about a heated discussion she had had with her brother during which he'd said, with great emotion, "You're just trying to prove me wrong!" His field of vision had become so narrow that he was only aware of how he was feeling. It never occurred to him that his sister was trying to make herself heard.

Your brothers and sisters may even believe that their preoccupation with themselves is natural and healthy. They may quote various pop psychologists to defend their positions. Since you pride yourself on being sensitive and considerate, you are a prime target for this sort of nonsense. "Maybe he's right," you think. "Perhaps I'm the selfish one." Your brother may believe that the best defense is a good offense and accuse you of having his moral deficits. Another possibility is that your sister, like Alex, says things for their effect, not because she believes them.

But you have to resist the temptation to blame yourself, and instead develop strategies for dealing with them.

Stand Up for Yourself

Sometimes, the healthiest way to handle a difficult sibling is to shift the blame from yourself back to the sibling who has been blaming you.

Blair, for example, routinely blamed her placid sister Melinda for everything. And Melinda took it—for a while. But one day she'd had enough. Realizing that she was being unfairly targeted, she wrote to Blair, "Your accusations and insults are unfair. I've been your biggest supporter in the family and have asked our brothers not to react to your moods and your selfishness."

Much to her surprise, Blair wrote back, "Let's stop this exchange of angry e-mails and phone calls and get back to being sisters." No amount of reasoning could have gotten Blair to this point. She needed to hear Melinda say, "I won't take it anymore."

As Melinda found out, holding your sibling accountable for her actions can be healing for both of you. Most people feel unhappy about the mistakes they've made and the hurt they've caused others close to them. And most are relieved if given the opportunity to make amends.

Work Toward Understanding and Accountability

In the introduction to this book, I said that as the healthier sibling, you would have to take the first step. This often entails telling your sibling how you've been hurt or why you are angry. You can make it clear that you require an apology.

Then, it's up to them to see their responsibility and to find some way to meaningfully apologize. Unless and until your sibling apologizes, there's really nothing you can do.

Of course, an apology without a change in behavior is meaningless. That's why I suggest that you accept the apology, but conditionally. Tell yourself that you're going to wait and see if your sibling repeats the offensive behavior. If he or she is a repeat offender, I strongly suggest that you tell him or her that you're accepting the apology but will be watching to see if there has been real change.

Action Steps to Deal with a Difficult Sibling

- Try to stay calm. To a person with character issues, everything is somebody else's fault. If you lose your temper or blast your sister with the "truth" of her insensitivity, you can be sure that she'll use that one indiscreet moment to justify future abuse on her part.
- If the character problem is mild, accommodate it from time to time. If your mildly narcissistic brother needs to be the center of attention, indulge him once in a while.

After all, nobody is perfect and such indulgence may help him to be nicer to you and the rest of the family.

• Whatever you do, don't forget that whatever your sibling says reflects his or her own viewpoint.

• Don't engage in character assassination. Remember that your sibling is still a human being. Be circumspect about your diagnoses. Remember that there are degrees of difficult personality issues, from the fairly harmless to the downright dangerous.

• Don't waste your time arguing. If your brother or sister has the sort of difficult personality traits you've read about in this chapter, you'll never convince him or her that your viewpoint is correct.

• Try to be generous, but be careful. Don't be taken in. When your previously untrustworthy brother convincingly says, "I've changed. Everything is going to be different now. It's a new me," wait and see if its true.

• To the extent that you hope for any change in your difficult sibling, think about behavior change, not personality change. Never do anything with the goal of getting your sibling to change his or her basic personality. That's a sure recipe for frustration.

PART 4

Looking to the Future

Chapter 11

Eighteen Ways to Help Your Children Avoid Sibling Struggles

"My brother and I haven't spoken for ten years. I don't want that to happen to my kids."

I've heard statements like this countless times over the past twenty years. When adults' relationships with their own siblings are not everything they wish they were, they often express anxiety about their children's future relationships. It was the distress of parents of young children over just this issue that led me to write my first book about sibling problems, *Beyond Sibling Rivalry*.

As you've read in previous chapters, childhood patterns of sibling conflict often continue to play out for a lifetime. This means that anything you can do now to enhance the quality of your children's relationships will benefit them for the rest of their lives. No matter how difficult your relationship with your siblings was or continues to be, there are many ways in which you can help your children get along better now and as adults.

The eighteen recommendations that follow contain a mix of "quick fixes" for sudden eruptions of sibling rivalry and more in-depth suggestions to change and improve the essential nature of your children's feelings about themselves and their relationships with their siblings.

1. Make your children's happiness a daily goal. *Self-confident children who have good relationships with their parents have very little reason to look for ways to make their brothers or sisters miserable.* Children with a healthy sense of self-esteem tend to cooperate rather than fight with their siblings.

On the other hand, children who are anxious about their self-worth, their place in the family, their acceptance by peers, their achievement in school, and, most of all, your approval are often unhappy in very fundamental ways. And it is this sort of fundamental unhappiness that lies at the core of most sibling rivalry in childhood.

2. Eschew comparisons. *Don't compare your children to each other, to your sibling's kids, to the neighbor's kids, or to yourselves as children.* It's very tough to convince your children that they ought to be cooperative and mutually supportive if they regularly hear you compare their intelligence, diligence, helpfulness, or personalities to that of others. While many parents know enough to avoid obvious negative comparisons ("Why can't you be more like your brother?"), they persist in more subtle comparisons. Referring to one child as the "athlete" and the other as the "artist," for example, encourages competition and comparison as children struggle to determine which attribute you prize more highly.

Even positive comparisons create strife. You may be tempted to say to your socially competent child, "It's great that you have so many friends; everybody can't be a math whiz like your brother." But this remains a subtle put-down. My advice is to tell your son that you're happy he has so many friends and then stop talking!

Another easy-to-make mistake is the "positive comparison"—"I wish your sister would learn to come home and do her homework right away the way that you do." Statements like this have many unintended side effects. The praised child may end up feeling guilty, or worried that she's being criticized behind her back. Avoid them along with all other comparisons.

3. Understand the difference between healthy competition and problem sibling rivalry. *As important as it is for you to avoid comparing your children, there's nothing wrong with them comparing themselves or competing among themselves.* In fact, it's a natural and healthy part of family life. So are disagreements. Children will always fight about whose toy is whose, who chooses what movie to watch, or who got the bigger piece of cake.

Think of the Williams sisters, Venus and Serena, who fiercely compete with each other for tennis championships. Yet as sisters they are very close and able to rejoice in each other's victories. My guess is that their father, who has been very actively involved in their tennis careers from their first days on the court, has consistently encouraged them to maintain a strong sibling bond even while competing at the highest levels of the sport.

Such healthy competition isn't limited to sports. I recently read an article about the Brown family—five siblings, ranging in age from fourteen to twenty-one, all studying piano at Julliard at the same time. It's hard to think of an area of professional endeavor more competitive than that of the professional pianist. Each of the Brown children is certainly aware of how few opportunities exist for classically trained pianists, and yet they get along well and are mutually supportive. No doubt their parents have instilled in them a commitment to the family as a whole, a sort of "one for all and all for one" mentality. They have taught their children that competition can be present even while closeness flourishes among siblings.

But sometimes healthy competition crosses the line and becomes more problematic. To be on the alert for the early warning signs of unhealthy sibling rivalry, ask yourself:

- Does one child go out of his way to avoid being with his sibling?
- Does one child appear afraid of another?
- Does your child insist that another child is your "favorite"?
- Does your child appear sad most of the time?
- Does one child *always* give in to the other?
- Does one child dominate family activities to the extent that other children can't get a word in edgewise?
- Does one child get angry when you pay attention to another child?
- Do they bicker all the time?
- Does it seem as if one child truly resents the other?

If the answer to any of these questions is yes, and the problem persists over a period of several months, think about whether the problem might be a symptom of a bigger underlying problem.

4. Model good behavior. *Children copy what you do, not what you say.* If you're concerned that one of your children seems to blame a sibling for everything, take a few minutes to examine your own behavior. Do you tend to blame your spouse, or other people in your life? In many cases, children adopt the behavior they see in their parents.

I do not mean to imply that every time a child is nasty to a sibling it means that parents are being nasty to each other. However, there have been many times when I've been asked for advice on how to improve a sibling relationship only to conclude that the marital relationship needed improving.

Be aware of how you speak to everyone in your life—not just your spouse, but coworkers, neighbors, relatives, and friends. If your children hear you jump into an evaluative mode whenever anyone's name comes up, or say critical things about other people behind their backs, they will copy you. If, however, they hear and see you give other people the benefit of the doubt, extend yourself to help other people, and avoid gratuitous criticism, they'll learn from that as well.

5. Be aware of imbalance and unfairness. *Not everything in life is fair, and when your child is angered by this, it's best to acknowledge it.* Resist the urge to say, "Life is unfair." It is—but that's not the point. Your goal is to help your child identify what makes his or her particular situation unfair.

Children complain about things being unfair so often that it's very easy to dismiss their complaints as "childish." They also use the "It's not fair!" strategy to try to get out of responsibilities, gain access to privileges, and manipulate parents. These complaints are not really so much about fairness as they are about things not going the way your child wants them to. "It's not fair" can be translated as "I don't like it!" or "I don't want to!"

Yet there are many times when things truly are "unfair." For example, suppose your son has very few friends and great trouble making friends, while his sister is the most popular girl in her class. It's not her fault—it's not anybody's fault—but it isn't fair.

True, these issues are not under your control. Neither you nor anybody else directly caused them, nor can you repair them. That doesn't mean that you can't help your child deal with this unfairness. Is your son angry because he wants to have more friends and tries so hard but has very little success? Find out what his concerns are and let him know that you understand and want to help. Even if you can't change things fundamentally for your children, you can make a situation better by listening and by providing practical help.

If your child is suffering from an inequity that is within your control—a coach who never moves her from the bench to the soccer field, for instance—then you can intervene directly on her behalf by either talking to the coach or helping your daughter develop strategies to resolve the problem on her own.

6. Have the courage to take responsibility for your mistakes. *When you make a mistake, apologize for it.* Children have generous spirits and are able to overlook even our more serious missteps if we accept responsibility for them.

Accepting responsibility entails two things: offering a sincere (and remember, children have built-in phoniness detectors; the younger they are, the more difficult it is to fool them) apology, and taking pains to not repeat your mistake.

7. Let them know that you want them to get along. *Don't assume that your children know that their having a good relationship is important to you.* Instead, take the time and make the effort to talk to them about how you want them to be as brothers and sisters. If you are about to have a second or a third child, talk to the older ones about what it means to be a big brother or a big sister. Take them to a sibling preparation class. Visit your library and take out some picture books about new big brothers and big sisters. Rent videos on the subject. Make a big deal out of their important new role in your family. Set the stage.

If your children are older, it's just as important to talk with them about what kind of relationship you want them to have. Tell them how you want them to be together as brothers and sisters. Talk to them about ways in which they will be able to help each other in the future. Tell them about famous and infamous siblings in history and the present: Cain and Able, Jacob and Esau, Wilbur and Orville Wright, Tom and Ray Magliozzi (Click and Clack, the Tappet brothers), Serena and Venus Williams, the piano-playing Brown kids.

8. Help each of your children discover his or her special gift. *Thanks to Alfred Adler, the physician who coined the phrase "sibling rivalry," we know that it's important to help children discover their gifts—that is, what truly makes them feel alive, what they have that they can contribute to others.*

Think about what your child is really good at, what excites him. Watch and listen to him. It takes both patience and a certain distance: you have to keep your own wishes and dreams for your child to yourself. Let your child talk about his interests, and reflect them back to him.

For many children, and adolescents as well the process of discovering a calling begins with self-definition: "I'm a person who likes challenges," "I'm somebody who likes learning new things," "I just love being around lots of people," "I love thinking about how things work." Some of these self-statements may eventually develop into careers; others may not. But what they have in common is that each focuses on a positive characteristic and a positive self-identity; each involves self-worth and self-knowledge. And though the goal may change, the process remains constant and will ultimately guide your child toward personal fulfillment.

9. Help your children develop the right kind of self-esteem. *It's possible to have good self-esteem and be entirely self- rather than community-focused.* Some children grow up feeling good about themselves and pay no attention to those around them. But for me, and I believe for most parents, the right kind of self-esteem means taking pride in being generous, compassionate, and helpful toward others; not holding a grudge, or speaking ill of other people; and treating other people—including siblings—as they would like to be treated.

10. Figure out what motivates each of your children. *Children have reasons for doing what they do that are not always obvious to us, and part of your job as a parent is to understand their motives.* Some children I've met seem to enjoy upsetting their siblings. In fact, some come right out and say, "I just like it when we fight." In cases like this, it's sometimes true that what the child enjoys isn't the fighting or making his brother upset, but the excitement, or perhaps the physical contact.

Once you know this, you can propose an alternative plan along with an incentive. For example, if children like to be physical with each other, you can suggest that every day that they refrain from teasing each other, they can engage in a supervised fifteen-minute wrestling match.

11. Don't be afraid to step in to resolve a fight. *Know when to intervene in sibling disputes and when to let them resolve them on their own.* I've met lots of parents who resist the urge to intervene even when they want to, and probably should. On the other hand, despite parents' concern that their attempt may actually make it less likely that children will resolve problems on their own, I've met very few parents who interfere too much.

Here are some guidelines that may help you decide when to intervene in your children's squabbles:

• The younger your children are, the sooner you should step in. Three- and five-year-olds simply don't know how to resolve differences on their own; seven- and nine-year-olds rarely do: they all need your help.

• If your children's conflicts become physical quickly, then intervene sooner rather than later. If you start to wonder if you should do something, you probably should.

• If it sounds to you as if your children are heading toward some sort of resolution, no matter how slowly, do nothing. It doesn't matter whether they get the problem solved efficiently or whether they reach the same outcome that you would.

12. Be positive. *Catch your children when they're getting along and acknowledge it.* We tend to ignore our children when they're good—which frustrates them—and notice them when they're misbehaving—which reinforces them in this.

To counter this, do the unnatural thing: overwhelm your daughter with your attention and recognition for being cooperative. If, for example, you think she's annoying her brother to get attention, flood her with attention when she's behaving well so that she won't be motivated to seek attention for negative behaviors.

13. Use discipline and punishment carefully. *No matter how carefully and consistently you try to emphasize the positive and to "catch them being good," there will be times when you will have to discipline your children.* When you do, follow these guidelines:

• Don't allow your emotions to match your child's. The more upset your child is, the more important it is for you to keep your emotions under control. If your child has just lost his temper and hit a sibling, or you, don't lose your temper and hit him back. This will only make matters worse by communicating that it's okay to hit people when you're upset. Instead, find a way to calm down yourself, then discipline by using a time-out or by taking away a privilege.

- After you've punished your child for a rule violation, don't mention it again. This means not talking about it with your spouse in front of your child. It also means not putting your child on the spot: "Tell your mother what happened this afternoon when she was at work." This sort of double jeopardy is unfair, it never helps and can have some pretty undesirable side effects. If your child feels embarrassed, upset, and angry about being confronted once again about her misdeed, she will focus on that "unfair punishment" instead of learning the lesson you were trying to teach.

- Use a time-out assiduously and carefully. Restrict its use to more serious infractions, such as fights that turn physical. If you overuse it, it will lose its effectiveness.

14. Pay attention to physiological factors. *Look for patterns in your children's behavior that you may be overlooking.* When our children are infants, we try to intuit what they may need: Does a fussy baby need a bottle? a diaper change? to be held? Unfortunately, we get out of this habit as our children grow older. But even school-age children need help in understanding their own behavior.

You may notice, for instance, that your school-age child always picks on her little brother shortly after she gets home from school. Maybe she's hungry—even though she doesn't say so—and needs a quick snack as soon as she drops her backpack. It's common for children to miss the early signals of hunger. Or maybe your children quarrel most at night, when they're sleepy. If so, an easy solution is to make sure they have less contact then. Another possibility is an earlier bedtime. Paying attention to these physiological problems can nip sibling rivalry in the bud.

15. Help your children resolve problems with friends and at school. *Sometimes problems from school or the* *playground spill over into your home life.* Just as adults sometimes kick the cat because they're frustrated with a coworker or a boss, so, too, children who are frustrated with friends or teachers take out their frustrations at home, where they know they're safe. It's not at all unusual for a child to tease a sibling because she was teased by a friend at school.

That's why it's important to get to the root of the problem. Find out what's bothering your child, and take steps to help her address it head-on, either with or without your help. This will have both short-term and longer-term benefits. Your child will feel immediate relief and so will not be as inclined to take frustrations out on her sibling. She will also learn that it's worthwhile coming to you with problems since you can actually help her resolve them. Finally, she will also learn the importance of finding the true source of problems.

16. Start good communication patterns early. *Teach your children to communicate with you.* Start at the earliest age and continue to work at it. Many childhood and adolescent problems, both sibling related and otherwise, can be avoided or quickly resolved when your children are in the habit of talking to you and when you are in the habit of listening to them. Some children are naturally talkative and will tell you everything that is on their minds. Others have a more reticent nature and need to be coaxed to tell you more than "School was okay." You can do a lot to help both kinds of children talk with you about their thoughts and feelings by being a good listener.

This is not an easy skill to acquire, but it is an important one and a useful one. Like real estate, listening well has three key principles: patience, patience, and patience. The more naturally quiet your child is, the more patient you will have to be. If your son, like many boys I've counseled, is more comfortable expressing himself physically, whether on the ball field or wrestling on the living room floor, it may take a while for him to become comfortable talking with you about his concerns. Here are some suggestions for getting physically oriented or otherwise reticent children to open up:

• Instead of asking questions, tell stories. Talk about how you used to feel at his age, or what happened to your brother when he was a child.

• Approach conversations indirectly. Even children who are not normally talkative will often spontaneously share ideas and experiences while riding in the car or during a halftime break at a basketball game. Sometimes simply not having to make eye contact helps.

• When you do ask questions, start with those that are easy to answer. Multiple-choice or true-false questions, even though they provide less information, are often easier to answer because they require less of your child. For instance, you can begin by asking, "You look unhappy. Did you have a tough day at school?" If the answer is yes or even a shrug, you can follow up with a multiple-choice question such as, "Was the problem with a teacher, or the work, or with the other kids?" Save the more reflective question—"What made it tough?"—for last.

17. Teach your children to manage their emotions. *Children who are able to calm down when they are worked up about something at home or in school are much happier with themselves, and as a direct consequence easier to be around and much more cooperative with their parents and siblings.* The stress-management techniques I described in Chapter 8 work for children, too. Many children love the whole idea of being able to control their breathing and pulse rates. (Some

214

children, however, become more anxious when they are asked to breathe deeply and focus on their physical sensations. If your child objects to the exercises, don't push him or her.)

If you find it difficult to learn the relaxation techniques well enough to teach your children, or if your child is truly anxious about something specific, such as starting at a new school or being caught in a thunderstorm, you may wish to set up one or two consultations with a child psychologist.

18. Set a good example. *Do whatever you can to get along with your siblings, your spouse, and your children.* Modeling is the single most potent way that you influence your children's development and behavior. Don't be afraid to let your children know that you have disagreements with your siblings from time to time, or that you have to work to resolve these disagreements. When you wonder if it's worth the effort to try again to connect with siblings, remember that no matter how things turn out, your children will learn from what you do. The best way for them to learn that it's worthwhile to extend themselves to their siblings is for them to see you do it yourself.

Chapter 12

Advice for Spouses, Partners, and Other Innocent Bystanders

The people who are closest to you are deeply affected by any event or experience that is important to you. If you are trying to get in shape, or lose weight, you can be sure that your spouse, partner, parents, and close friends are feeling the effects of the project as much as you are. When you go to the fridge for that midnight snack, should they remind you of your diet, look the other way, or join you for a bowl of ice cream? Couples routinely get into arguments about just this sort of situation, as anyone who has either tried to diet or been with someone who is dieting knows very well.

If something as mundane as a diet can affect relationships in such a problematic way, it's not surprising that your conflicts with a sibling, as well as your attempts to improve that relationship, readily reverberate through your closest relationships.

I wrote this chapter to provide some support and guidance for your partners and spouses. I encourage you to share it with them.

Paulette's Story: "My Spouse Doesn't Get Along with His Sibling"

Paulette had worked very hard, on her own and with me, to improve her relationship with her older sister. Even after years of effort, it was not perfect, but she was satisfied. There were fewer arguments. They actually enjoyed spending time together. They spoke regularly on the telephone and were generally mutually supportive.

Her husband Walt's relationship with his four siblings was noticeably lacking, at least by Paulette's' standards. He thought of his sister Natalie, the one closest to him in age, as a two-dimensional cutout, only concerned with gathering as many material possessions as possible and with self-aggrandizement. He saw her only every other year. But he had even less of a relationship with his brother Billy, whom Walt considered to be "strange" and to whom he hardly ever spoke. Though he felt a bit more warmly toward his two youngest siblings, Ellen and Steve, they lived several thousand miles away.

All this caused Paulette a great deal of distress. She admitted that she wasn't sure if it would have bothered her so much if she hadn't put so much effort into developing a good relationship with her only sibling or if she hadn't from time to time wished she had a brother or two herself. She wished she could help but wasn't sure how or where to begin.

Here are some suggestions for what you can do to help your spouse or partner:

- Be patient. Remember that there are decades of history behind your partner's difficult relationship with his siblings. It may feel as if you've been encouraging rapprochement forever, but in actuality it's only been a small fraction of the time that led up to the problems.
- Balance acceptance and gentle constructive criticism.
- Be supportive.
- Don't make it your "mission" to improve your spouse's or partner's relationship with his or her siblings.

- Remember that your partner's or spouse's sibling is not your sister or your brother. There's a fine line between being concerned and caring about this relationship, which is helpful, and responding to every disagreement or conflict as if it were happening to you, which can be more hurtful than helpful.

- Be understated. Your spouse's or your partner's feelings are probably raw. Try to be subtle rather than blunt. Don't say: "You really should reach out to your brother." Instead, wonder aloud if perhaps there might be some way to reopen communication.

- Consider asking your spouse to do something for your sake if he's not interested in doing it for his own benefit—but only do this once.

- If your partner doesn't welcome questions about his motives and feelings, he may be more comfortable in speculating about his brother's or his sister's motives and feelings. This can often get at the same issues.

By following these suggestions, you will most likely be able to help your spouse resolve issues with his or her siblings. However, there are some situations that require a little more attention—perhaps the feelings are too negative, or have gone on for a long period of time. In cases like this, you will need some new insights and skills.

Maggie's Story: "I Had to Wait for the Right Time"

Maggie had been looking for an opportunity to help her husband, Charles, forge a better relationship with his brother. After dancing around the topic for years, she finally came right out and told him how much his continual bickering with and complaining about his brother bothered her. Like many of the distressed spouses I've talked to, Maggie was an only child who often wished she had siblings. It upset her deeply that Charles seemed to want to push his brother away. When Maggie told him how she felt and that she wanted to help him resolve his differences with his brother, her husband accepted this to please her—at least that's what he told himself.

Months after this discussion, Maggie happened to be nearby when Charles received a call from his brother. She wasn't sure exactly what motivated the call. Neither could she tell exactly what they were talking about. What she could tell was that the tone of the call was closer to neutral than usual. It sounded like she'd been given an opportunity to advance her cause. She would have liked to call him away from the phone for a minute to give him a pep talk but knew very well how much that would irritate him so she wrote a little note and slid it onto the table next to him. It contained only nine words:

BE
interested
curious
supportive
neutral
appreciative

At the bottom of the note she added: "You're doing great!"

This technique won't work for everyone, but it worked for Maggie and Charles and it may work for you. What made it effective was the fact that Maggie and Charles were patient, waiting for just the right moment to be supportive and positive.

In other situations, a spouse may need to take a more active, interventionist role in order to heal or avert sibling disagreements.

Peggy's Story: "I Told My Husband He Couldn't Play Favorites"

When Barry's older brother turned sixty, he had a huge party. Family members came from all over the country. Barry had always looked up to his brother and would not have missed the party for anything. He, his wife, and their children traveled from Philadelphia to Des Moines for the party and had a great time.

A few years later, Barry's younger sister Joanne turned fifty and a big party was planned for her. This time, Barry was ambivalent and hesitated, blaming overwork and expensive airfares. But the truth was that he and his sister had never been really close and he just didn't want to go.

Ruth, his wife, saw the potential for trouble. "It's difficult," she told him, "We went to Barry's party. If we don't go to Joanne's, it will seem like a snub. It will be hard to explain. I truly believe you'll regret it if we don't go." She wasn't strident but neither was she shy about expressing her opinion.

Thanks to her efforts, they went to Joanne's party and enjoyed it. More important, though, Barry felt that it marked a turning point in his relationship with his sister, who was moved and appreciative that he'd come so far to be with her. Barry said that in retrospect it would have been a big mistake to have missed the celebration and that it might have created even more distance between him and his sister. Far from minding Ruth's intervention, he felt grateful to her.

"My Siblings Don't Get Along with Each Other"

Sometimes, when sibling problems exist between two people in a family, it leaves the other siblings perplexed and distressed. Amy, for example, was the kind of person who could get along with everyone. But for some reason, her sister

Rachel and brother Mike never got along. Now in their thirties, they'd been estranged since they were teenagers. Mike insisted it was because Rachel was such a "pushy and bossy" older sister throughout their childhood that he couldn't possibly feel close to her. Rachel told Amy that she was ready to make amends whenever Mike was, but that he had said so many nasty things about her that he would have to at least apologize first. Both were convinced they were right.

After being placed in the middle for too long, Amy called me for a consultation. How could she help her siblings reconcile? Some of the things that Amy, and you, could do are:

- Ask your brother and sister, "If there was something you could do to improve your relationship, and it was fair for you to do it, and you believed that your brother or sister would appreciate it and might possibly reciprocate, and it was not too difficult, expensive, awkward, or time consuming, would you do it?"

- After your sibling answers your question in a way that is at least close to the one you hoped for ("Well, I guess so" or "Maybe"), he or she will probably add all the reasons that it wouldn't "work." Don't pursue this. Let the conversation drift to another topic. You've planted the seed and now you have to wait.

- Don't push the issue. If there's any hope for change, it's going to take some considerable time; if you show impatience, things will certainly backfire.

- Keep your expectations low.

"My Grown Children Don't Get Along"

As the years go on, parents have less control of the relationships among their grown children—but that doesn't mean they have no influence. In fact, they probably have a bigger impact than most realize.

Many of the issues that are important to work through when children are young—competition, fairness—remain important through the years. Parents who don't pay attention to how they treat their grown children can inadvertently contribute to difficulties between the siblings themselves.

For example, Henry Smith, a very successful business-man in his seventies, came to see me because he was per-plexed about the intense conflicts among his two sons and two daughters, all in their thirties and forties. He cared deeply about them all and was genuinely upset about the lack of connection among them. What he didn't realize was how his handling of money—and he was extremely gener-ous—exacerbated their difficulties.

His oldest daughter spent more than she had and needed regular infusions of cash from her father, his mid-dle son was frugal, and his youngest son lived well but within his means, as did his youngest daughter. Henry had evolved a system whereby he gave differing amounts of money to each child, based on his understanding of his or her financial situation. The elaborate calculation backfired—naturally. The younger children all resented the older ones.

When we first talked about this, Henry was surprised and disputed my view of the situation. As we looked in detail at the pattern of his gifts, however, he saw that his gifts to his children revealed a startling lack of equity. He was following the old socialist maxim, "From each according to his abilities to each according to his needs," but this did not fit the reality of his family. Eventually, he realized that the gifts had mean-ings for all his children.

My advice? Keep everything equal.

"I Want to Help My Grown Children Get Along Better"

What role should parents play in their children's lives once the children become adults? There are many theories. I'm not sure there's any one right answer. What I do know is that it's emotionally impossible to stop being and feeling like a parent and equally impossible to stop caring about how grown children get along. You may not have as much influence as you did when your children were young, but that doesn't mean that you are powerless.

On the contrary, you can help your children—no matter what age—get along in many ways. Here are some suggestions:

• If you know one sibling is trying to improve her relationship with another, acknowledge and encourage her effort.

• Prepare her for the fact that some of her efforts may be met with disappointment and rejection.

Afterword

In the previous pages you've read about all kinds of sibling relationships and all kinds of sibling problems, from the very mild to the very severe. You've also learned techniques for managing your feelings, for improving communication, for being appropriately assertive, for finding ways to enhance your own self-esteem by "doing the right thing, and for stopping yourself from saying or doing things that you may regret later." Now it's time to put your new learning to work. As you being to apply these techniques, bear in mind that none of the stories you've read will exactly mirror your relationship and relationship difficulties with your sibling or siblings. What is more likely is that specific aspects of some stories, rather than the complete stories, will resonate with your personal experiences. Something that one of the siblings in these stories said will remind you of something your brother or sister said, even though they may have said it in a totally different situation.

As I conclude this book, I want to share some thoughts with those of you who have repeatedly tried and failed to heal broken relationships with siblings, only to be disappointed, or worse. I'm thinking particularly of those whose siblings are more like those you read about in Chapter 10 than others you encountered in this book.

To a large extent the benefit of trying to improve your relationship with your sibling comes simply because you are trying or have tried. It's tempting to look to your sibling's response to your efforts as final exam grade. That's fine, when your sibling responds positively. But, as you read in Chapter 10, your brother or sister may have character defects that make it close to impossible to bridge the gap between you. Unless and until he or she changes profoundly, your efforts will be just that: efforts. Churchill was right of course in admonishing us to never give up. On the other hand, there is a time to admit defeat, while taking some comfort in having done one's best. My strongest image for this comes from the time I spent teaching pediatric residents and fellows caring for patients at The Children's Hospital of Philadelphia. There were times that despite the best efforts of the best doctors, children did not get better. The same is true of close relationships: there are times when despite your most genuine and best efforts, you will not be able to salvage your relationship with your brother or sister.

For others, those for whom it make sense to continue to work toward genuine dialogue and genuine healing of a fractured or uneasy sibling relationship, remember these points:

- You can change only yourself, but sometimes that's enough. Many battles with your sibling will be averted when you begin to respond to the opening volley differently from the way you have in the past.

- Set your sights high, but keep your expectations as low as you can. Here is how I think about it: your expectations are goals you have decided you "must" achieve. If you fail to achieve them, you'll feel that you've failed. The lower they are, the more often you will experience success. Setting your sights high, on the other hand, means that you are striving for the best possible result, all the while realizing that you may not reach it.

Index

Cain and Abel, 209
"catching children being good,"
 211
categorical thinking, avoiding,
 123–26
change over time, 127
changing others, attempts at, 3
 myth sibling needs to change,
 13–15
changing ourselves, 3, 129
 as sufficient to begin the
 process of changing the
 relationship, 13–15
character, 182
character assassination, 12–13,
 183, 200
childhood:
 destructive entitlement
 resulting from, 137–39
 helping your children avoid
 sibling struggles, see sibling
 struggles, ways to help your
 children avoid
 memories from, influencing
 adult relationship with
 siblings, 58–59
 parentification in, see
 parentification
 patterns of relating established
 during, reverting to, see
 patterns of relating
 established during childhood,
 reverting to
 revisiting, with self-awareness,
 57–59
 sibling rivalries originating in,
 21–26, 58
communication, 67–89

action steps for improving skills
 of, 89
of appreciation, 78–79
complaining, guidelines for,
 77–78
embracing differences in styles
 of, 70–71
guidelines for talking to your
 sibling, 73–77
identifying your style of, 72–73
listening, 79–80
nonverbal, see nonverbal
 communication
process, being aware of, 82–83
sarcasm, 73, 75–76
teaching children good patterns
 of, 213–14
thinking before you speak, 73,
 76–77
touch, 88
understanding sibling's reality,
 73, 74–75
understanding styles of, 67–73
compassion, 25, 144, 210
 for mentally ill, 197
competition between siblings:
 difference between problem
 sibling rivalry and, 205–206
 finding a new way of relating as
 adults, 115
 parents who compared siblings,
 91–98
 protracted, 93
complaining, 152
 guidelines for, 77–78
con artist, 188–90
constructive criticism, see
 criticism

reverting to childhood roles, *see*
   patterns of relating
   established during childhood,
   reverting to
differences:
   in approaches to relationships,
      allowing for, 25
   in communication styles, 70–71
   embracing each other's,
      106–107
   in style, avoiding overreacting
      to style, 110
disciplining your children, 211–12
disputes, intervening in your
   children's, 210–11
"doesn't everybody feel that way?"
   thinking, 127
drug abuse, 175–77

eating habits, depression and,
   166, 168
Ellis, Dr. Albert, 122, 159–60
embarrassing of sibling, avoiding,
   110
emotional abuse, 24–25
empathy, 141–43
enabling, 179
ending a relationship with a
   sibling, 107–108, 195–96
energy, depression and lack of,
   164, 166
entitlement, 18
envy, *see* jealousy
estate, settling parent's, *see*
   favorites, parents playing
estrangement, permanent,
   107–108, 195–96
excluded middle, law of, 124, 125

excusing difficult personality
   type, 196–98
exercise, 166
exoneration process, 97–98
expectations:
   about your childrens'
      relationships, letting them
      know about, 208–209
   holding on to, 128–29
extended family, 143

fairness rather than feelings,
   focusing on, 56–57
family counseling, 100–101
fault finding, invisible loyalty
   and, 96–97
favorites, parents playing, 23,
   91–98
   avoiding making comparisons,
      204–205
   awareness and, 94
   bonding and attachment and,
      94–95
   exoneration process, 97–98
   favored sibling, harm to, 92, 205
   getting over, 92–93
   less favored sibling, 92
   parental loyalty and, 94–97
fear, physical sensations of, 54
feelings:
   being in charge of your own, 51
   "difficult," acknowledging,
      51–52
   "discounting," 54
   expressing, 116
   focusing on fairness rather
      than, 56–57